NEIGHBORHOOD OF STRANGERS

O.Z. Lysiak

Neighborhood of Strangers
by
O.Z. Lysiak

Paperback ISBN 13: 978-1517182564

Cover & Interior Design:
Pamela Marin-Kingsley, pammarin-kingsley.com

For more information, please contact:
olehzenonlysiak@gmail.com

Dedicated to Peter Harvey Spencer
(January 18, 1939 - February 15, 1999).

Table of Contents

Acknowledgements

Special thanks to: Christina Anne Peterson for her support and patience, Charlie Alexander for proofreading and home made jam, and Jackson Ordean for research and tenacity.

Reasons

Recently I've wondered what possessed me to return to San Miguel County. Simple reasons surface immediately: money and a woman.

The north coast of Oregon was home last fall when my friend Claudia Hoffman proposed we do a show at her home on Wilson Mesa. I was intrigued, delighted and we pulled off a doozy.

The October 9, 1994, afternoon the show was held was splendid, sunny and spectacular. The mix of people Claudia invited was an elegant one - knowledgeable, adventurous and good-natured all.

Monika Callard catered the affair. I would have showed for the food alone. Many of the people who came did just that.

The event was an extraordinary white witch brew. I made more money in one afternoon than in the entire year and, to top it all off a good-looking tall woman whisked me off to dinner...

I gave away the trailer I was living in on the coast, packed everything I owned in the back of a '79 Ford short bed pickup and moved to Norwood where I opened a studio. Things didn't quite turn out as planned. Promised commissions from Telluride art aficionados fizzled, and in a few months I was writing for a newspaper again.

What a turn of events! I was going to turn the art world on its ear and here I was being the voice of the rednecks. I'm old enough to where the twists and turns on the road that's become my life no longer surprise me.

I avoided Telluride like the plague. The confusion in the streets was appalling, the Rasta geeks a joke, development outrageous, hard to find a bartender I knew. The situation was totally out of hand.

What I failed to remember was I originally arrived in town with shaved head, gold earring, ivory bracelets, a purple satin cowboy shirt with white piping, pearl snaps, fresh from the Renaissance Faires in California.

Raymond Hughes gave me a job hosing down Main Street every Friday morning, flushing out the sewers every spring, driving the water truck to keep the dust down, digging up sewer breakdowns. We built the water system.

Dirk DePagter gave me a job jack hammering Main Street to install the Victorian streetlights. We'd fire up Ray Fancher's ditch-witch by dragging it down the street and days it was too cold to get the digging started I'd pour 10 gallons of gasoline into the ditch, light it and jump back. The flames would leap up towards the second story of the shops. We came up with the concept of immigrant engineering.

LaMont Woozley gave me a job running the shop in back of the original Telluride Sports. I'd get the rentals out in the morning, make repairs, and ski The Plunge from 11 to 2 every day of winter.

I got married at Alta Lakes, built a house in Placerville, ran Trusty Trucking hauling construction trash to Nucla, trading salvage for what I could get, selling cordwood in Telluride. Fred Williams and I did Philly Steaks at the festivals for years. I was divorced here.

After I was arrested for high seas highjinks, Mike Ritchey wrote me up in his fledgling paper. I wasn't happy making the paper in a felonious capacity but what he wrote was accurate. Some things a guy can depend on around here.

I spent more of my adult life here than anywhere else in the world. I could have stayed in the Galapagos, La Paz, Manila, Labuan, Kota Kinabalu, Munich, Cologne, Copenhagen, Oslo, Stockholm, Helsinki, Paris, Barcelona, Toronto, Montreal, Vancouver, Anchorage, Accra, Panama City, Quito, Guayaquil, Cabo San Lucas...

No matter where I was in the world I'd always wind up back here, an extreme place, which caters to extreme personalities. Suits me fine, despite the latest series of bitches.

I had a hand in making this town what it is. I'm not ashamed. It's one hell of a place.

This morning I'm out with Willy, my dog, walking the edge of San Miguel Canyon, wondering what the hell I'm doing here again dancing the economic samba.

I notice scarlet paintbrushes, white barrel cacti blooms, the San

Juans to the east, Lone Cone to the south, the La Sals to the west, skies clearer than crystal, the muddy San Miguel roaring below.

A golden eagle circles overhead, scopes out the canyon's edge for breakfast. I step into the shadows of a pinion, lock onto the golden. He makes a few more passes, folds his wings and dives. I follow him for seconds as he plummets out of sight. The last thing I remember is how the sound of his blitzkreig descent rips through the morning.

I whistle Willy in and head home, doubts dispelled, reasons all around me.

THE SAN MIGUEL COUNTY POST

Peter Spencer and I seal the deal with a handshake on a cold, gray afternoon in an empty lot next to the San Miguel County Post's offices. Laughing, we cross the street to the Lone Cone Saloon to celebrate. A few tequilas and beers later we go to work.

I cover Norwood politics, town board meetings, water commission meetings, regional water board meetings, school board meetings, high school sports, Rodeo Days, horse racing, Christmas pageants, art shows; Telluride politics, the county cop shop, county commissioners meetings, county planning board meetings, regional transportation board meetings, festivals; interviews, commentary and opinion, do all the photography and write a weekly column.

A year reporting for The San Miguel County Post is the best job of my life, every day with something interesting to do. Peter Spencer is a pro with a sense of humor, loves a long shot and is a joy to work with. We have disagreements. If he even hints at changing a comma in one of my stories, let alone one of my columns, I kick open the Post's door and we take it to the empty lot where I rant and rave. Peter listens until I run out of steam and assures me he'll change everything back to the way I wrote it. We go across the street to the Lone Cone Saloon, have a shot and a beer and go back to work. Of course he never changes anything. By the time the paper is out the next day I'm calm and see his point.

Gwen Davidson, the Post's assistant editor continually requests I use the spell checker on my computer. Since there's no time for rewrites and copy I turn in is written in one take, I consider her nagging request but refuse because the spell checker doesn't work in context. It becomes a joke between us.

Eagles winter in the San Miguel Basin. I submit photographs of eagles every week until Peter hollers, "Uncle! No more eagle shots,

OK?" I submit photographs of kids, geezers, the Lone Cone, camels, pigs, bucking broncos, sheep, buffalo, cattle, every manner and sort of critter imaginable.

Once all my other copy is turned in, I write Fishing With Uncle O, a weekly column, some of the best writing I've ever done. I go fishing and write about it, my job. Can life be any better?

The Post is a modern version of a 19th century paper produced on very sophisticated computers and printed on a classic newspaper web press using soy ink. There is a lot of hauling around of newspapers in this process, what with circulating in 3,000 square miles of one of the country's most thinly populated areas and mailing subscriptions to far away places.

The San Miguel County Post started publication on May 4, 1994. In his first editorial, which became his weekly Fearless Leader column, Peter writes about the original Norwood Post.

"These newspapers duly recorded the milestones of daily life, births and deaths, marriages, celebrations. Sometimes an ink drawing of the latest fashions from the east would amuse, a serialized novel entertain. The latest news of national politics (not more than a few days or weeks after the fact) would be the talk of the café, and a shooting or a report of a rustling would bring outrage or excitement. Advice from the vet or the local doctor would be carefully studied, recipes and crafts from local homes would be clipped out and saved. The best horse in the race or the best time in a calf roping would always rate the front page, with little or no attention paid to gossip or scandal in distant cities. Feisty editors would rail against some perceived injustice, and opinions were sometimes challenged with fists or even bullets.

"In an age when mobile populations and scattered families are the norm, cohesiveness of rural communities is as important as it was a century ago. The original Norwood Post was published from 1912 to 1938. A revival of the traditional rural newspaper can be a centerpiece in maintaining a sense of connection to one's neighbors and the community as a whole. To that end, the revived Post will attempt to chronicle, report, educate and entertain.

"The Post believes that most of what is important happens outside the halls of government and although we will cover meetings and politics as part of our obligation to inform the readers, we will devote our most enthusiastic coverage to our children, our community and our daily lives."

Neighborhood of Strangers

The San Miguel County Post, in its first year was criticized for not covering enough government meetings.

"Of late," Peter writes, "in the heat of political controversy, we feel we have covered too much government activity. We will endeavor to correct that imbalance this year"

In 1926, the following was reported in the original Norwood Post: "M.O. Ballard took over publication of the Norwood Post on February 1, but declined to make any rash promises as to what he would do thereafter. He merely stated that he would work for the best interests of the community and he had long ago given up the idea that a breathless world waited to the stroke of his pen to determine whether it could go on for another seven days, which indicates rare judgment and discretion.

"One very poor man can promise more than a score of good ones can fulfill and while our hopes have a certain bearing on the scope of our accomplishments, it's what is done, not what is intended that counts."

"We trust that The Post has not disappointed Mr. Ballard," writes Peter.

Peter and I discuss getting health insurance for The Post's employees, acquiring local newspapers and a radio station. Peter helps me buy a house in Norwood by manipulating financial information on my mortgage application. It works. If I'm saddled with a mortgage I'll need a job and stay at The Post.

I morph into The Post's cultivator of controversy by writing commentary and opinion after I write straight news stories about the meetings and events I cover. My news stories are not necessarily balanced but my commentaries are incendiary. Letters to the editor complaining about my commentaries and opinions play perfectly into the cultivating controversy plan. Circulation grows and people take notice. The Post is the voice of reason in San Miguel County, balanced between the hard core rednecks, farmers and ranchers of the far West End and the overbearing, high dollar liberals in the far East End, a neighborhood of strangers.

To me it's about the people, the land, the tradition and heart of the county, not the new money, the promise of development or the prospect of big bucks rolling in. I know where I stand in relation to development and big money. The people I interview write their own stories in their own words. I listen, transcribe and provide introductions and endings.

Like all good things it comes to an end, more quickly than I would have liked. Life happens.

FISHING WITH UNCLE O

Friends

If it weren't for friends I never would have accomplished a fraction of the things I've done, or seen as much of the world as I have. I also wouldn't have gotten into nearly as much trouble.

Getting out of trouble builds character and enlightens a person to the fact that all is never totally lost. Hope, hard work and the light of understanding conquer most anything short of a bullet through the brain.

Luckily, my friends are artists, writers, pirates, lawyers, cowboys, bikers, smugglers, hookers, debutantes, editors, adventurers, ex-cons, rascals, rednecks, scalawags, working women, men, and peripheral types who put off proper, politically correct, holier-than-thou stalwarts of mainstream society.

The people who have befriended, helped, and enlightened me enriched my life. If it weren't for the wild women and men in my life, I might have turned out to be a "suit" with a totally boring life and an equally boring outlook.

Fat chance. Some wait for the stars to guide them. Dirk DePagter told me others create their own stars.

Just last year, a couple good friends in Basalt, one who owns and the other who manages Frying Pan Anglers, traded me an entire fly-fishing outfit for one of my mobiles deifying fish. Now I'm equipped with fishing gear the likes of which I never could afford and they have a mobile the likes of which has never been seen before.

Art Rowell took time to introduce me to the joys of fly fishing 30 years ago on the Roaring Fork. We hiked over Conundrum Pass to Crested Butte and back. I spotted a pool with rainbow trout in the shadow of the Maroon Bells, whipped out my telescoping spinning rod and caught three in the span of a few minutes with a Daredevil lure.

Neighborhood of Strangers

Art gave me hell all the way back to Aspen, swore he'd convert me to fly- fishing. We went out on the Roaring Fork. Art rigged me up. I snapped off the first few flies he tied on. Eventually I stopped snapping off flies, calmed down and hooked into a nice fish. I worked the fish to the bank. Art unhooked the fish. He let it go. I saw no reason to go to the trouble of catching fish if you're going to let it go. I wanted to cook and eat my trout. Art's fly rod and reel wound up in the Roaring Fork.

Ray L'Hommedieu gave me his grandfather's split-bamboo Montague and an ancient Union-Made brass reel. Pete Symes took me out on the San Miguel and patiently taught me the basics. Pete taught me the barrel knot, which I now can tie in a blizzard by feel. I gave the Montague to Art as an apologetic gesture for tossing away his rod on the Roaring Fork. I had things to learn.

Soupy Campbell taught me you've got to be smarter than the worm when you're bait fishing. Soupy is from Mississippi. He taught me the art of catching, handling and cleaning catfish. Soupy introduced me to the filet and release philosophy of conservation.

Marcus Coldsmith taught me if you're going to catch fish you've got to have bait in the water. Marcus is absolutely the best fisherman I have ever had the pleasure of fishing with. He will fish for anything, anytime, anywhere, with endless enthusiasm. Bass fishing wouldn't exist in my fishing lexicon if it weren't for Marcus. He taught me the improved clinch knot for which I'll be forever grateful.

Gary Waldon taught me how to rig multiple hooks for saltwater fishing, how to dive for abalone. From Gary I learned things I can't mention here. He'll be out of the joint soon.

Ron Brown, who unfortunately is no longer among the living, taught me how to gather ghost shrimp for cabrilla fishing off estuary beaches in Laguna Manuela, Baja. He taught me to tie imitation ghost shrimp from minute gull feathers for halibut in shallow estuary waters. Ron called me a farmer because I horsed fish. He shamed me into a softer, more artistic, more effective approach. I miss Ron Brown and occasionally take a wineglass of tequila, something we shared at the end of every fishing day.

Larry Allen is absolutely the best mechanic I have ever known, a Hell's Angel who taught me the trucker's hitch, without which my life as a rigger would have been hell. He also taught me that a guy's got to have a bigger truck if he's going to carry more stuff at a point in my life when a backpack seemed too much. Larry introduced me to the joys of Chevy 235's and 4 speeds.

There's more but what I'm getting at is it's a person's heart that counts. You love somebody in spite of who they are. That's real.

Friends don't always stick around, especially the adventurous ones. What you share stays with you. You can't take that to the bank but you can depend on it.

Grenades

Could be it was action movies with gratuitous violence I've seen over the last couple of decades. Could be it was the training I received from Uncle Sam. Could be it was the mean streets of Philadelphia I grew up on.

Maybe it's common sense and decency have me reaching for a wish grenade to toss at the fool standing in the river decked out in the latest fly fishing regalia, fly rod in one hand, cellular phone in the other pressed to his ear.

Last summer Roudy, a local outfitter, had a group of tourists out on an evening ride. They were looking forward to seeing elk. Silently, they ride up on a herd. One guy's cell phone beeps. He answers and starts talking. The elk immediately split. Roudy takes the guy's phone, smashes it on the ground. Seemed like a good idea at the time. Seems like a good idea now.

A pal of mine works for a bucks-up Texas lawyer. The lawyer calls his mega-square-foot palacial digs above Telluride from his Texas headquarters, has the boys meet his personal Citation jet at the Telluride airport. The boys drop what they're doing, fire up one of three loaded 4X Suburbans parked at the joint (the lawyer also keeps a couple brand-new Harleys just in case somebody wants to take a ride) and drive up to the airport to pick the lawyer up. The jet lands and the red carpet rolls out. Out stroll a Harlequin Great Dane and a Labrador Retriever. No lawyer, just dogs from Texas. We've got plenty of dog shit already without importing more.

Makes me wonder if the money is worth the price. Are these people strung out or simply nuts? Who needs it?

What motivates people to come to our back yard and bring all their big city foolishness with them? Who needs a cell phone on the river? Who needs a phone on horseback? What the hell is the point? If you can't live without your phone, STAY HOME or have the courtesy to stay in your car or in your room.

The brochures tell the suckers the fishing's great. It's a hell of a lot less great since they started polluting our rivers. Population pollution is a bona fide category. There are more people on the water than ever. Since this is America I guess I'll have to let'em but it certainly is nice to imagine vaporizing one of those suckers every once in a while.

This is another sales job on an unsuspecting public. The rubes buy it. They're just so SPECIAL, as special as their Visa or MasterCard. Hello.

They come here to vacation, unwind, go for it or whatever they can conjure for their dollar. They could at least leave the bullshit behind instead of hauling it around for the rest of us to deal with. We can send them a bumper sticker approximating their being here. They can send us money. Do we want these fools running loose around here? Or do we want them to stay home and send us their money? I know what I want.

Perhaps we could convince the Nature Conservancy, Sierra Club, and whatever other environmental outfits out there to draw up a new set of politically correct rules for fools who come here to pollute our back yard.

Huggers already hustle the fools for dough so maybe we could get them to instigate a program where they can send videos of what is precariously still here for donations to keep it that way as long as those who donate don't come as part of the deal. We'll include a bumper sticker says these people are environmentally aware and actually did something about it by staying home and taking care of their own back yard.

They could at least draw up a new set of guidelines telling other bucks-up huggers to leave the damned phones and idiotic electronic claptrap home when they come visit the remaining vestiges of wildness. An occasional grenade might do some good.

What the hell's the use of saving whales when you're freaking out the elk with telephones?

Struggle

Art Rowell and I fish the Frying Pan, something we unfortunately don't get to do very often since we're always working.

After a few small holes, Art suggests we go towards Ruedi Reservoir and fish a killer hole he knows. We arrive, Art points out the lunkers in the hole. We wade into the current.

We aren't there five minutes when a brand-new Range Rover pulls up, a woman dressed in the most current fly fishing regalia gets out, walks over to the hole and casts. I bite my tongue and keep fishing.

A few minutes later another SUV pulls up, a guy gets out, walks over and he starts casting. I ask him what the hell he's doing. The guy looks at me like I'm nuts and keeps casting. I put my fly rod down and walk over to this intruder to explain to him in no uncertain terms he isn't welcome at this hole and fishing etiquette requires he at least ask if it's all right with Art and I. We were there first and have a plan in mind how to fish the hole.

Art sees what's was happening, puts his rig down, sprints over and asks what I'm doing. I tell him I'm going to tell the son of a bitch and his girlfriend they're not welcome at the hole. At this point I'm speaking in slightly agitated tones, fists clenched.

Art asks me to chill out. We know each other over 30 years. He tells me these people are customers at the fly-fishing shop where he works and would I please not cause a ruckus. I assure Art there will be no ruckus soon as I throw both assholes in the river, a moot point because while I stew more people arrive like a herd of fishing sheep, ridiculous. Why would anybody want to fish this way?

When I was a kid we played basketball on the playground under the elevated between the projects and the neighborhood. We had black kids, white kids and Hispanics on the playground. If you wanted to play you asked if it was OK with whoever held the court. If you didn't, it was an invitation to get your ass kicked. At least we had a sense of courtesy and treated each other with respect born of necessity. The fools at the fishing hole had neither, needed a good ass kicking.

Art insists I cause no trouble for customers. I don't blame Art. It's not his fault. Fishing is his living. The shop employs several guides. A job is a wonderful thing. Fishing as business in southwest Colorado has changed the nature and quality of fishing as recreation and pleasure. More and more and more people move into areas that were secluded and hard to get to a few years ago. My idea of a quality fishing experience is not a line dance with a bunch of neoprene-clad yuppie chumps at the local hole.

A few years ago you could fish any hole on the river in silence and solitude. Today you have to get past the lineup of SUV's every quarter mile or so. Holes and sections of the river, which were hard to get to and known only to locals are now exploited by fishing guides who give up the good water for a buck. I'm not against them making a living but I am against losing the good holes.

In late winter when the ice recedes you could be assured of getting the river to yourself. Today you follow tracks in the snow. There's more pressure on the trout population every season.

Stretches of river are devoted entirely to catch and release. The people who perpetrate this on us are interested in catching as many fish as they can and letting them all go. It's business. When fish are handled over and over there's a good possibility they'll die if not handled properly. I've seen fish belly up in the river and it makes me angry. What is it that makes a person need to torture fish over and over? A hooked trout is fighting for its life, doesn't realize you're Marquis de Sade in chest waders toying with it.

I don't necessarily agree with what's happening but I don't have to. All I have to do is figure out a way to live with it. Crowding on rivers is a reflection of what's happening in the valley, the country and the world - too damned many people!

I don't like the politically correct liberal bullshit perpetrated by each succeeding wave of know-it-all urban refugees but I don't have to. All I have to do is find a way to do something about it.

Good thing Art was along the day I encountered the crowd at the hole on the Frying Pan. If instinct prevailed, I would have punched the guy in the nose and thrown him and his girlfriend in the river. I would have visited the Pitkin County Jail (which is a very nice jail, as jails go) and Art might of lost his job. I wouldn't have learned anything.

I understand we need to live together although some of us need to live less together than others. This conflict forces me to come up with creative solutions to get what I want. As long as there's struggle, there's life.

Transition

He smells transition, feels change in the season, first solid rain in months awakens him long before daybreak. No getting back to sleep, a multitude of things course through the darkness on the wings of his somnolent imagination.

He's aware of the smooth give and creak of the old pine tongue-in-groove floor on the way to the kitchen in half-light. After putting on water for coffee he returns to the covers and dawn-dreams his way into daybreak.

Files and gas can stand ready next to the saw in the shop. The chain gleams, oiled, sharpened, adjusted. He'll gas up the truck before he leaves town in case it turns to adventure today.

The incense-like smell of beetlekill spruce fills his dreams as orange, cream, pink and pale gray rounds drop off felled standing dead. There's loading and stacking. If he's lucky the road won't be the consistency of mucous by the time he's ready to leave.

He saves the spare for the top of the rounds in back of the battered old Jimmy. If he doesn't a flat is assured. The bump in the turn for the bridge usually jars the spare off and it rolls down the embankment into the creek. The climb out of the creek is a chore, packing the wheel. With a full load the front tires hardly touch the dirt. Makes steering tricky.

May as well pack the .22 in case there's grouse on the menu today. He spotted a bunch on the way home from town. Soon as he puts down the saw for a break, sits on a stump at the edge of a clearing to have a long drink of water, spruce chickens take off with knife-sudden whirrrrs. He spends the next half-hour checking out treetops for little gray heads peeking to see if it's safe. Just about the time he's ready to give it up because he figures he imagined the grouse, one'll come out and it's a crisp, small caliber invitation to dinner.

Neighborhood of Strangers

He seeks boletes, oysters, chantrelles along the road to the wood stash. Still early for inky caps poking up though the hard pack alongside the gravel. 'Caps won't be out until deer season and he's done cutting wood. And then there's the pinon nut harvest. No use going into the forest that time of year unless you're prepared to shoot back. He stopped shooting deer and elk some years ago when the idea crossed his mind to shoot Texans instead. Now he keeps his wilder ideas to himself.

His thoughts turn with the change in weather, about what needs to be done on the house and the shop. If he's lucky there'll be huge snowfall and plenty of water for fields in spring and summer, in ditches for asparagus, running rivers and plenty for fish. First there's cracks need filling and the roof on the shop leaks.

Time to check pipes and ready the stove and make sure the heat tape works on the water pipes so he doesn't come home to a skating rink in the kitchen because the pipes burst and the damned floor froze over like the first winter in Telluride long before his hair turned gray.

And there's a ton of stuff to do on the truck. He got the heater to work by fixing the cable controls but it's time for replacing the wipers and getting those pesky squirters to work. A lighter grade oil change is in order and it's time to check the antifreeze before the first really cold night.

His Sorels are in good shape since he bought a new pair last winter. No need for patching but a good, solid greasing is called for. A couple of pair of wool socks would be handy.

Best part is this is the season when big German Browns hit with signature fierceness no other fish in the river displays. You know when a Brown takes your fly. No doubt about it, you're in for a tussle, something actually wild you connect with.

Water for coffee is ready. May be enough wood in the stash to last. The road'll be incredibly greasy. Browns could be biting today. The rod and fishing gear are already tucked away in the truck.

Swallows

Following swallows at daybreak, the first cast cuts through flat-water mists and   lands the #20 pale dun midge on Miramonte Reservoir's rippleless surface.

The swallows feed on the hatch in an utterly joyful display flashing split black tails and tiny gray, yellow, orange chests and bellies. Honkers sound raucous warnings at my intrusion and swim off into the mist. A coyote choir wails on in elongated yelps and yips like Sunday morning gospel up a draw back of where I'm casting. Two pairs of mallard wings rip overhead. A swallow dive bombs my fly and veers away in a minute fraction of a second in search of tastier pursuits.

The water's smooth as oil on a glass tabletop. The sun is up over the ridge and weekend fishermen are still in bed. It's cold enough to make me put my hands inside my pockets between casts, not a trace of dust on the dirt road after the first rains in quite a while. Smells verdant, fresh and raw.

Each cast is effortless, elegant, fluid without wind to fight. Day-glow orange line pays out in sinuous perfection, landing the fly more lightly than a conspiratorial whisper in a touchy situation.

A hike along the eastern shore provides no clues to rising fish although the swallows seemingly are gone berserk. They land on sage-brush carcasses long drowned and recently exposed. And each few steps I take, the swallows jump and flurry off along the shore in search of drowned sage perches like feathered, breathing ornaments atop a graveyard full of memories.

The glitter of the frost along the cracked and caking mud disappears the closer I get to the inlet at the south shore of the reservoir. The sun is well above the ridgeline and my hands come out into the warmth. Crawfish antennae, claws, carapaces in mottled reds, browns, creams and blues testify silently to the luck of the draw.

Still no rises. I cast on. The midge, tiny as it is, is hard to spot atop the glare. Blaze orange hunters' caps dot the shore across the water. Bait fishermen set up along the west shore at the base of the peninsula.

Steve Steed and I caught plenty of Miramonte's muddy tasting late summer trout in just the spot the orange caps are set up in. We'd hunker down below the bank and cast into the windswept and snarly void. We'd always bring a twelve-pack. It was impossible to talk Steve out of drinking Coors and drink real beer instead. Sometimes we'd bring a pint of downstream brandy because we knew it'd be a long and windy ordeal to wait the lake trout out into having a taste of what we hoped would be something a fish without respect would eat. We just as well might have tossed Twinkies out for bait.

In early spring we hiked to the southern inlet just as the ice came off the lake, as soon as the road was passable and fish in goose down jackets, wool trousers, caps and gloves, feet toasty in Sorels. The fish would bite on anything, hungry after a winter under the ice.

We'd get a fire going to keep warm and grill fish under 16 inches in a day-long hot lunch program while we whacked scores for the smoker. Our antifreeze of choice that time of year was mescal con gusano. The lucky one who got the last swig usually got the worm. I remember one of our pirate fishing crew in Muslim prayer pose on the floor of the shower after one of our infamous Miramante debacles while the rest of us fried trout and sent an emissary off to the liquor store in Sawpit for re-supply. We were younger and Sawpit had a liquor store then.

Steve helped me build the smoker the Miramonte trout were destined for. We found an old Kelvinator refrigerator, cut holes in the top and bottom for 6" stovepipe, shot a few holes in the fridge with a .22 for ventilation, fitted the pipe with dampers, along with a cap on top. The bottom we connected to a 55-gallon drum used for a cooker. Dirk DePagter provided apple wood from an old orchard in Delta for smoking wood and Mike Baer concocted a brine divine. The smoked trout were legendary in the neighborhood and we took the opportunity every spring to catch a barrel full to smoke so everybody would get some. It never lasted though because the word got out and we were out of smoked fish in a less than a week.

Cold smoking took three days of constant vigil. The fish marinated in Baer's Secret Brine overnight. Then they were lovingly hung in the smoker off the racks, seared with original flames and soothed in cool apple wood smoke until they flaked off the bone in moist, delectable mouthfuls.

Steed also turned me on to deer and elk hunting and the joys of bushwhacking the back roads of San Miguel County. Steve, Tom Spyke and I began the hunting season every year with dove, band-tailed pigeon, grouse and mushrooms before moving on to deer, elk, and later duck, pheasant and bunnies. There was never a lack of game in the freezers in our homes. We worked and played together; hauled our spoils out of the woods and onto the dinner table. We never had a lot of money but there was always something delicious to eat and plenty of everything worthwhile to share.

Steve died last year in La Junta, where he quarterbacked the high school football team. He's buried with his own and we were lucky to have known him for the short time he was with us. I miss him. I miss Tim Woozley and Randy Higgason. Seems the only time I ever get to see my old pals anymore is when death brings us together, a sign of the age. Janis was right, you've got to get it while you can.

Emerging from my sentimental reverie I realize I'm up to my crotch in Miramonte, boats trolling, mists long gone, swallows explosive in alarming grace. I'm back from the past and wiping away tears, not a rise in sight. I roll up my rig and hike back to the truck.

While taking off my waders a white-haired old-timer approaches me on his way back from the crapper. He tells me he's been camped here since Wednesday with some good hits on red and white spinners while trolling. The bait fishermen have been pulling in some lunkers, he claims, but he caught a 17-incher last night. The only time the fish are rising is at dusk, immediately before dark and only along the southwest shore of the island just off the channel by the dam. We talk for a while and I tell him I'm heading home because I've got a lot of work to do.

"Wish I could," he replies and walks down to his trailer.

I pack my fishing rig into the Jimmy and concoct plans for breakfast, a lot of stuff left to do today.

Thankful

The day is warm, cloudless, soft and perfect. I'm knee-deep in the San Miguel, with occasional Thanksgiving traffic touching the periphery of my concentration as I cast over the long deep pool under the Norwood Bridge.

People in cars above hurry to share moments with loved ones, watch the Cowboys wipe the Astroturf with the Chiefs, stuff themselves with stuffing, trimmings and the inevitable main course.

Warm weather in late November has extended the fishing season for a glorious couple of weeks. I'm thankful and appreciative. The kids are thankful to be out of school, the ranchers are thankful for not having to feed their stock this late into the season, and anybody with a lick a sense is thankful not to be fighting weather on their way to grandma's.

Skiers and realtors aren't thankful because there's no snow on the mountain. Tough. With a little patience they'll get theirs.

The blue dun hatch is strong but I can't get a fish to take my imitation. They'll slowly roll up to the surface and act like they're thankful after dinner because they're stuffed with flies.

Second cast after a switch to nymphs I hook up with a German Brown and we're in for a fight. Nice fish! He measures sixteen honest inches, brings to mind the fishing in this river before development and prosperity forced us to fishing in preserves. The guys who made the dough developing now fly to Alaska to fish "unspoiled rivers." The San Miguel's still a damned good place to fish if you can wait out the summer clutter of Range Rovers or Grand Cherokees every quarter mile, the hoot and holler of rafting tourists and commercial guides giving up the good holes for a buck. What the hell - everybody's got to make a living.

Next fish is another brown and so it goes Thanksgiving Day in all the good holes I remember on my favorite river. This is the best day fishing of the entire year, like the stockers disappeared and all the real, wild natives of the San Miguel had at it. What a day to share with the slicks, riffles and blessed solitude in the canyon.

I truly am appreciative because until Thanksgiving Day the most memorable catch of the season had been an case of poison oak contracted somewhere around the confluence of the San Miguel and Dolores fishing for catfish. The catfish skunked me that day but I found a few good holes for skinny- dipping.

Soon enough the winds and snows erase all trace of human tracks along the river and the pace of fishing pales. The quality of solitude is amplified between the river's freeze and thaw, time to give the local fish a rest save for memories.

I make it home in time to see the Cowboys whip the Chiefs, enjoy the company of family and friends, delight in the feast complete with wild and local trout I graciously invite home for dinner.

Sunday

Here the river runs deep, swift, tricky, a dicey place to fish. The trout feed on the hatch of the day in quiet pockets of water amid opposite bank rocks.

I rig with nine feet of 7X tippet and a #22 midge. Finding secure footing in the rip and roar requires patience teetering on the edge of balance. I find my spot and cast to the opposite bank over the current's roil. A trout comes out from under the rocks to look my presentation over. I miss the strike, and again.

I hook him next strike. He goes deep to an eddy close by the current. I play it gingerly with the 7X tippet. He's a good fish, I can tell by the bend in the rod. I don't want to lose him.

Once he's close to the surface I work him across the current. He's almost across when he bolts for the eddy and bottom again. A half hour struggle and I have him in my net.

He's a beautiful 19-inch Rainbow. I gently slip my hand under his belly in the water, remove the hook, work him back and forth until he comes around, and in a flash, he's gone.

The sun barely peeks over the edge of the canyon, almost eight o'clock, plenty of time for breakfast in town. The day is off to a great start, Sunday race day at the fairgrounds. I'm photographing the action.

I walk rather than drive to the track, a good decision. Good angles and unusual perspectives are the order of the day when I check out the starting gate. I find unusual perspectives all right. Tom Bennett, Larry Williams and Dave Williams provide rare insights and perspectives on the personalities, horses and history of racing in San Miguel Basin. Much of what is said shouldn't be repeated. The starting gate crew is a can-do, good-natured bunch of ex-wild men who now claim to be mild men. I'd like to believe them, no matter what anybody says.

It's such fun at the starting gate I never make the grandstand. I barely make it home. Good thing I didn't bring my truck.

Tom Bennett shares an insight into the enthusiastic approach the Williams clan brings to living. "Give a Williams a vehicle and a full tank of gas," Bennett says, "and you've got a dangerous situation. They'll run out of vehicle long before they run out of gas."

Doing research takes its toll, a hell of a way to make a living. Some Sundays are tougher than others.

Stress

The stress of dealing with the lack of available holes on the San Miguel drove me to seek action elsewhere. Lately, the road from Keystone Hill to the Norwood Bridge resembles an elongated yuppie parking lot. I was ready to hit the road.

Compounding the stress is a low-water year with trout holing up and hugging bottom at the approach of every Orvis-equipped imitation flanger. Fishing in low, clear conditions like this requires patience beyond belief, stalking skill and finesse in presentation.

A fishing trip away from home was in order. I called my good pal T.W. (Third World), an ever road ready, non-whining, literate, globe trotting fishing enthusiast, photographer, conversationalist and all around good guy. We tossed some fishing and camping gear in the back of the pickup and took off to fish the Dolores.

An inordinate amount of traffic occupied the road. We had forgotten it was the height of tourist season, spots we cultivated over decades of regional exploring were occupied by RV's, campers or desperate fishermen. The Dolores was lower than the San Miguel. We laughed it off and drove on. After all, we are intrepid adventurers and small setbacks don't phase us.

The loveliest part of the drive turned out to be the girls who hold up traffic signs at numerous highway construction hold ups all the way to Dolores. Someone with actual taste and a discerning eye hired these delectable asphalt maidens. Our undying thanks to this person, whoever they are. There wasn't a dog in the bunch. The scenery around here is like wallpaper anymore, especially on a sticky, hot afternoon when you're forced to wait. The addition of well-equipped highway maids with endearing smiles makes all the difference when you're on the verge of turning surly.

It was the wrong afternoon to be jumping barbed wire fences with No Trespassing signs. We waited until we got right outside Dolores and fished a flat- water stretch which looked totally fished out and impossible. T.W. caught one 12" rainbow in two hours. I exhausted all my best flies and managed two non-hits but several definite swirls.

We journeyed on and visited with Taz Vass, who grew up in Telluride, got an English degree from Ft. Lewis College in Durango and now owns the food market in Dolores. I remember him as a kid but now he's taller, bigger and presented me with more questions about regional politics than I could answer. In the not too distant future I expect Taz will be mayor of Dolores or president of an African country.

T.W. and I retired to the Hollywood Bar, a local watering hole where I drank as a tree planter 22 years ago. We planted trees up Taylor Creek Mesa and came to town on days off for a beer and a game of pool. The local loggers eyed us warily but we took no crap, a lot of us home from a highly unpopular war. Eventually we worked it out, like reasonable rednecks, some longhaired, some short.

We ordered beers, T.W and I, and talked philosophy, a lot of which was justifiably drowned out by the jukebox. We tried to come up with a plan, which would get us away from the crowds. The tail waters below the dam at McPhee were down to an unbelievably low cfs. If we went there, we'd encounter less water and more flangers. There was a possibility of heading up the West Fork, past Dunton and fishing the headwaters and beaver ponds but lack of water and an over abundance of visitors precluded that. In the morning we decided to go to Durango.

Imagine our surprise when we discovered the Animas way low also. We talked to a good pal of T.W.'s, Mick, who owns the fly fishing shop in Durango. Mick told us that there was good rookie fishing on the Animas and the tail waters below Navajo Dam on the San Juan if you could put up with the crowds. We talked fishing for a couple hours and took off for Silverton and the Miner's Tavern, which is also the American Legion's Post 14. I just had to buy a bumper sticker there which states: "EARTH FIRST, We'll Mine The Other Planets Later." By this time it had begun to rain and neither of us had brought rain gear. When did it last rain?

Fishing was out of the question. We followed flatland drivers, you know the kind who slow down to a crawl on the curves and accelerate as soon as there's a passing lane available. Cars coming down from Molas Pass were laden with hail. I made a mental note to fix my heater. Summer is over. There was at least an inch of hail on the road at the top of the pass. We passed on Ouray and headed straight for the True Grit Cafe in Ridgway. There's been a power of yuppification in that town and the True Grit resembles that remark.

What I learned on my two-day loop is I should have stayed home, fished my own river at night after the flangers and weekenders were done. There's good company right here and the tequila selection is certainly a hell of a lot better.

Deals

Like many propositions, expeditions and deals do, this deal started over beers at the Lone Cone Saloon.

Dead Reckoning and I were discussing boats at the bar. We hadn't seen each other in nearly a decade. Boats were always our favorite topic of discussion along with women, money and exotic places around the globe.

Dead Reckoning had been skippering a yacht off the coasts of Central and South America for the last eight years. He'd come back to the area on urgent business. I was glad to see him. He put on a little weight but it made him look prosperous. His wit and generous smile were a welcome change from the usual bar fare.

He told me about an octoroon cook he employed on the yacht for several years. When they met in Venezuela she was barely 16 years old, 6' tall and from his graphic description - a knockout. He was sorry to see her leave several years later.

Dead Reckoning and I met one night over 20 years ago when he showed up at my door in Placerville and asked if I'd help him move some telephone poles that evening. It seemed like a reasonable request, the beginning of a friendship that continues today. He and I managed multifarious projects and established Trusty Trucking (& Midnight Salvage). Things were much looser in the county in those days and an ambitious and energetic guy, who could keep his mouth shut, could do all right for himself. We did all right.

We were engaged in a discussion about the pros and cons of wooden sailing craft when I told Dead Reckoning I had sent off for plans for a 19' wooden gunning dory I wanted to build.

"Why do that," he said, "when I've a got a wooden dory in California you can have. I haven't done anything with it in nearly ten years. It's at a friend's house. I'll call him and tell him you're coming to get it."

We discussed the particulars, made a deal and shook hands. We come from a generation where your word is your bond and a handshake seals the deal.

Dead Reckoning moved to Nevada in the spring where he was supposed to be carpentering for a rich uncle somewhere around Las Vegas. You never know with him. He's one of those rare people who move in and out of your life but inevitably move on. You're always happy to see him again and you learn to smile when you see him go.

I was committed to driving to California with my sweetie and her kids to celebrate a family Christmas in L.A. She and I dropped the kids off at grandma and grandpa's and took off up the coast with paperwork for the boat and trailer.

The dory had been sitting in a yard in coastal Northern California for many years. Her cover was torn, she was flooded in the stern, a little ragged, in need of TLC and paint but fine. Her lines were classic. She was one hell of a score. It took about an hour to check and pack the bearings, hook up the running lights, lash down the tarp and get a 1 7/8" ball at the local car parts store to fit the socket on the trailer and we were on the road at dusk, back down the coast like the experienced hit-and-run masters of the Great American Highway we are.

We stopped for a celebration a couple hours later at a seafood roadhouse with plate after plate of fresh oysters washed down with cold California chardonnay. I took all this in as a good omen.

Morning found us within earshot of relentless Pacific surf. We spent the night in the back of my Ford under the camper shell. A walk on the beach and we were off for another round of oysters and char- donnay for lunch.

After a huge Christmas celebration with my sweetie's family and the last Chargers' game of the season in San Diego we packed up the kids and the dory and made a burn run straight back to Telluride.

The dory got parked outside my shop in Norwood and life went on. Since the trip to the coast had exhausted whatever meager finan- cial reserves I had, I had to get a job in the extreme West End as the voice of the rednecks. It was fun for a while but like most jobs in the West End, didn't pay enough. There was money enough for sandpaper but not enough for varnish and paint. I sanded the dory under a make-shift tarp all through snows, which lasted into June. Unsuccessfully, I tried keeping the dory dry and iceless prepping her for the day when I had enough money to buy proper paint.

Tired of fighting the weather, I got a job in the Mountain Village doing custom condo bondage log stairs for a sleazeball developer. Now I could afford paint and varnish. I ordered them through the West Marine catalog. Not much time available for boat sanding with the demands of the job, I finished the dory in a hurry.

I had a new shop at the old slaughterhouse outside Norwood thanks to the kindness of local sculptor David J. Williams. The last coats of paint were applied as we prepared to launch the dory at Miramonte Reservoir soon as the weather cleared.

The first time we launched her off the new ramp at the east end of the reservoir, she immediately took on water. I figured as soon as the wood swelled, she'd tighten up. I was right. The dory was designed as a gentleman's sailing/rowing dory with a centerboard well, mast step, rudder, tiller, as well as oarlocks for rowing. She came equipped with a sail, mast, boom and rigging. This was a lot of regalia to pack around for an afternoon shakedown cruise on Miramonte so I left most of the esoterica home and rigged to see how she'd row. She rows like a dream, tracks like a freight train.

My sweetie and I rowed over to the far and usually deserted end of the lake, landed in mud and dense vegetation, stripped down and went skinny dipping in the balm of early afternoon at 10,000' in the San Juans.

The first couple of feet of water were warm enough but anything under that invited immediate waves of goose bumps. It was one of those "Me Tarzan, You Jane," afternoons.

We boarded our vessel and continued around the lake. My sweetie kicked back topless in the boat, out of sight of the campers and fishermen. I was content to row her around the lake for as long as she could stand high altitude sun on sensitive regions of her torso not accustomed to being exposed outdoors over the course of a murderous winter.

After decades of rowing craft designed specifically for whitewater I remember thinking that the dory was kind of a pansy boat. She was designed for Sunday cruises on calm bays and all the yachty regalia seemed superfluous. But she was a lot of fun to row around Miramonte and I came back several times to fly-fish or row around.

The centerboard well never quit leaking so I figured what the hell, let's see what this girl will do in whitewater.

Fisher Towers rise directly off the desert floor, sanguine minarets above the Colorado River, in full view of the peaks of the La Sals at Hittle Bottom put-in on the River Road to Cisco.

We put in shortly after daybreak while the river is silent, before the clamor of outfitters' rafts and passengers destroy the solitude between Hittle Bottom and Moab.

Serena has the oars of her newly rebuilt and refinished dory, the Emotional Rescue, locked under her knees while she rolls a handmade. Tina tightens her PFD (personal flotation device, we don't call them life jackets), jockeys for a comfortable spot in the dory's bow. I row. The cooler is strapped down in case of mishap. Feels good to be on the river.

The previous evening in Serena's yard we discuss what stretch of river we should run and decide to do the daily. I don't know how the dory will perform in whitewater. The daily has several rapids, none life-threatening, and will be a good shakedown cruise.

Serena takes the lead after the flat water stretch tucked up to the small cliffs river right before she disappears into the channel between the rocks on the first rapids. Doesn't look like much but any small mistake can ground you on a rock with the force of the entire Colorado coming down on you. We follow Serena's lead, hug the wall until we see an opening and go for it. The water is high enough we can't make the rocks out until I feel a scrape left side, adjust with an oar and we're through the worst, riding out the roller coaster of the current's tongue, laughing, soaked, exhilarated.

Next rapids are no big deal. We make adjustments and trim the dory. I row, Tina bails, feeling good, secure in our PFD's, happy our vessel is river worthy.

White's Rapid is the biggie coming up. Serena again takes the lead since she's run this stretch of river countless times. The waves are larger but we survive without hitting anything although we take on serious water.

In White's you have to watch out for eddies after the run out. If you're not careful and stray out of the current, eddies can suck you down. Been known to happen to even the most experienced river runners who let down their guard.

We land, roll the boat over, dump the water back into the Colorado and prepare for an easy cruise through the morning. The worst over, the dory handles like a champ.

Rocky Rapid comes up, where the river spreads and runs shallow for several hundred yards. Halfway through the rapid our dory grinds to a halt, spins across the current. I dig the upriver oar in to adjust our attitude. The oar catches in rocks and snaps. The dory rolls over. I watch Tina launch headlong toward the river. The dory lands on top of me. I come up downriver, immediately lock onto the gunwale with one hand, grab an oar with the other and scramble upriver of the dory to keep from getting caught between a rock and a hard place.

The dory drags me over the rocks. I hold on. A huge wall comes up fast, which the entire Colorado slams into on an immediate left turn. If I let the dory go there's no need to tell this story, she's kindling.

Tina is clear of the rocks in the Emotional Rescue. I slide the oar I'd hung on to into the dory and swim with everything I have to keep my dory off the wall. We slide through in the current and are dragged into another set of rapids. I keep her off the rocks again. Another set and I'm looking for a place to swim her in to shore.

Serena spots a beach downriver and pulls out. I swim in bruised, beaten, battered and not grinning. First time out on the river and I nearly get my sweetie drowned, almost destroy my boat. No way to know how much of a beating I took because I'm numb.

The upswung bow piece is broken off, the keelson is broken in two places, there's a break in one of the lateral rib sections, one of the vertical curved ribs is broken, both oarlock sockets are ripped out, the oarlocks are bent, the transom is broken and there are separations along the gunwhale and floor.

We load into the Emotional Rescue, look for a place to take out before we encounter more rapids. My dory on a tether, I'm in the bow making sure she doesn't gouge Serena's. I ward off the bow of my rig. A protruding copper ring shank rips through my thumb. Both women know me well enough to let me alone to scream out frustration, humiliation and pain.

The girls drop me and my mess off, happy to get away from the black clouds I conjure. I consider smashing the boat to bits with rocks but drag it to the highway instead. You can cook bacon on the sand. I have no shoes since they drifted downriver when the rig went over. How I didn't lose my wallet and keys is beyond me.

Tina doesn't lose her cool, doesn't panic and does well. I have the boat, my wallet, keys and things are looking up. This isn't a total disaster. I wait in the shade of a cottonwood a few yards from the road when Tina and Serena show up with my Toyota and trailer.

The three of us haul my battered dory to the road and load her onto the trailer. Thumb throbs like hell. There's cold beer at home. The possibility of improving the situation, although slim at this point, exists.

We check the dory at Serena's, determine the keelson caught in the rocks, causing the problem. I should have known better than to try and take a bay rig like this through whitewater. Somebody with more sense wouldn't have tried it.

"The difference between you and them," Serena offers, "is you have the balls to try it."

The Land Cruiser dies at the top of the hairpins above the Colorado border. I put my fist through the windshield. Luckily I don't have a bigbore gun along or I'd have blown holes in both the car and the boat. The points worked shut. Less than a year later, after adjusting the points countless times, I buy a distributor to remedy the problem.

Tina and I miraculously are still together. The dory is almost patched and we grow more alike each day, held together with faith, screws and epoxy, keelson's history. I fashioned a replacement for the broken rib out of it.

Enough

Greens in the big holes turn blue and deepen, riffle rock rusts and oranges sharpen and clarify as winter winds rip through what remains of brilliant yellows in branches of huge cottonwoods along the banks. Stark, gray, gnarled, leafless behemoths let the contrast of dark fir and spruce play against sanguine canyon walls.

Hunters from all over the world come here to ply their deadly craft, celebrate ancient Scythian, Celt, Visigoth, Cherokee rituals. They no longer sing songs of victory around the fire although they're in touch with atavistic stirrings. Storytellers regale comrades with tales of the hunt, the kill, prowess of the mighty, power of the seasons, cyclical realities of life and death.

Each hunting season since I moved to Colorado I filled our freezer with elk, venison, grouse, duck, rabbit, pheasant. We lived on game, depended on it to get through winter. Those were different times.

We hunted together, hauled game out of the mountains, our families skinned and butchered carcasses, shared in spoils. We never went without. Today fences and no trespassing signs indicate we should avoid places we hunted. A hell of a lot more people are here now with strange ideas about what's right which they unfortunately bring with them.

At timberline above Wilson Mesa, we park below and three of us hike through dark timber the day before opening. We pack sleeping bags, pads and tarps, Snickers and cans of sardines, a rifle apiece with a full magazine of ammunition.

I nestle into the root system of an enormous spruce for the night. The elk should come up the draw below. The faintest stirrings of light break to the east, hellacious cold when I wake. I dig my hands deep in the sleeping bag for woolen gloves, wait and listen for elk moving towards tree line, wool watch cap down along the bridge of my nose. The sleeping bag is past my lip as far as it will go, the tip of my nose sticks out, the only cold part of my body. The .270 is under the tarp, close at hand, ready to go. A thin layer of snow covers everything during the night.

At daybreak I imagine I hear something. Then all hell breaks loose, the retort of high-powered rifles like a vicious ambush in a full-scale war. I don't dare stand up but dig down into the root system more deeply, reach for the .270, rest it above my head like I'd been taught in the U.S. Army. If any rounds come my way I'll let it rip and face consequences later. I decide I'm through hunting big game.

Years later, working offshore, I'm at dinner with a dozen Texans bragging about hunting exploits in my neighborhood. One of them asks if I hunt.

"Nope," I reply in curt, Gary Cooper fashion.

The Texan wants to know why.

"Because I'd rather kill Texans," is my reply.

Lately, I judiciously pick times to fish in solitude because the rivers are so overrun. I haven't shot a bird in years, not since my good dog Butkus died.

Deschutes

Quicksilver-skinned river rips emerald to cobalt.
White-capped swirling wind gusts weave through
yellowed reeds. Driftwood smoke unveils a ghostly
belly dancer sinuous above the flames. Sun streaks
orange traces on empurpled clouds. I cook twisted
multicolored macaroni over hissing coals, toasty
to the roar of rapids come tomorrow.

There was a decision to be made quickly at the Hood River turnoff on the backside of Mt Hood. The girl hitch hiking to Hood River looked good at first glance, tall with thick blonde braids to her waist, wearing a patterned wool ski hat. That's all I saw.

My foot was off the brake, onto the clutch as I shifted into fourth gear and put the hammer down for the Warm Springs Indian Reservation and the Deschutes River.

Winter on the coast in Tillamook had been rainy, foggy, and I was trying to shake the blues. First thing that occurred to me was a trip in the desert and the Deschutes runs along the eastern boundary of the Warm Springs Indian Reservation in north central Oregon and empties into the Columbia River.

The Orca, my 18' fiberglass red and gold sea kayak was strapped to the roof of the pickup, life jacket and gear stowed in the back and I was ready to go, having read a couple of paragraphs on the Deschutes in Soggy Sneakers, an Oregon river runner's guide.

Arrangements had been made for a shuttle and I was launching the Orca when the shuttle driver showed up. I handed over the keys to the Ford, gave him some money, slid into the kayak and was gone.

It felt great, back in the cockpit of the Orca, low in the water, paddle blades slicing the river's surface in rhythm, glistening with flashes of droplets dripping off the smooth, white fiberglass edges. The early afternoon sun warmed my brilliant blue poly-pro-gloved hands.

There had been snow on the road from Rhododendron through Zig Zag, past Government Camp and Mt. Hood onto the desert. It was mid-March and there likely weren't going to be many boaters on the river this time of year.

The Orca and I floated under the Oregon State Highway 26 bridge and the road to Madras. The buildings on river right grew sparse in the first couple of miles. River left was the boundary of the reservation and the Warm Springs Indians had saw fit to put annoying yellow NO TRESPASSING signs every 200 yards along the riverbank.

Ignoring the signs was hard to do. I can only assume these people were pissed off about the last time we all played cowboys and Indians.

Five miles downriver there were railroad tracks and farmland river right and those damned annoying yellow signs river left. There was nothing I could do about it so I looked to the desertscapes past the bank, listened for rough water ahead and paddled downstream, hardly any need to paddle since the Deschutes runs along at a considerable clip. Every so often I'd dip a paddle or touch a foot control to adjust the rudder, bring the Orca a few degrees to either side and keep her nose downstream and in the current.

It was a lovely way to spend the afternoon. We encountered a few sets of rolling rapids three to four feet high, a pleasant ride and an early shakedown for the rig. Everything was copasetic and it was getting time to find a spot to camp for the night.

River left, of course, was out of the question so that narrowed it down some. I found a spot on a big bend protected by what looked to be sugar pines, set up camp, cooked dinner, had a couple Oreos and settled in to the sound of Whitehorse rapids a mile or so downstream. The Oregon sky was clear, stars out in force, with only an occasional coyote howl to break the river's song. I checked Polaris before I closed my eyes and next thing I knew it was morning.

Heavy clouds filtered occasional splotches of sun and I broke camp in a hurry. I heard the thundering of Whitehorse rapids long before I saw them. I pulled out a couple hundred yards upstream and scouted.

The main chute of Whitehorse was narrow, sandwiched in between massive rocks with waves over ten to fifteen feet high smashing through a roiling trough. Not a good idea for an 18' fiberglass boat designed to track straight lines over long distances of open water.

I opted to slip past the rocks on the left and avoid total disaster. There was another option open. I could have unloaded the boat and portaged downstream but I'm a stubborn goon and I wasn't going to let the river humiliate me.

When the Orca spun broadside, the force of the Deschutes rolled and pinned me underwater quick as lightning. I ripped out of the cockpit, hanging on to the paddle, grabbed hold of the bow grip and we all smashed downriver through rock gardens boiling with near freezing water. I absorbed multiple shots until there was occasion to regain my footing and slowly I worked my way over to the left bank, the hell with the Indians.

The Deschutes had torn out the seat, paddle rest and some of the deck rigging. I made a fire, warmed up and unloaded the Orca. Of course everything was soaked. The clouds had gone black and it started to rain. I rigged up a makeshift seat, taped over the holes and cracks with silver duct tape, loaded back up and put in.

More rapids. I was in the main channel on a long right hand bend when the nose of the Orca shot straight up and she landed backwards and upside down once again. No problem. I knew the drill from a mile or so back.

Actually, there was a slight problem, boulders the size of houses across the Deschutes three hundred yards downstream. I swam for all I was worth and twenty yards before the rocks crushed us I touched bottom exhausted, numb and exasperated. I sat on the Warm Springs shore and started to laugh. It was raining harder than it does back in Tillamook, the river had kicked my ass, I was on the wrong bank, now the back hatch cover was gone and a vision of two long blonde braids appeared just to taunt me.

In a few minutes I had a spot high up on the bank, the tent up, firewood gathered and a reflector built in front of the tent mouth. It took a while to get the fire going but I managed by rigging a tarp. Hot chocolate was next on the agenda with a dollop of brandy to sweeten the stakes.

Neighborhood of Strangers

By next morning the rain had subsided and I hung gear out to dry, rigged a hatch cover out of my rain jacket and shock cord and was gone before noon and the Injuns could find me. There was no need to fish—it was one of those trips.

It was time to cut losses, can the bravado, get real. I found a small settlement downstream and carpenters doing a remodel. They gave the Orca and me a ride to the highway.

I swore I'd be back but never did it. I repaired the Orca and sold her to a girl from Washington.

Remains

Hundreds of water spiders ride soft current swirls in the shade under the bridge. Refractive patterns reflect translucent yellow Jello lace against soldierly, geometric, weathered steel beams. Not a nibble in two hours. Beer's gone.

Ten-ply rubber squeals against soft blacktop on a scorcher of an afternoon. In minutes he's on the dirt below the flume along the red rock before the confluence. The San Miguel runs sparse, shallow, with pale green algaed stretches between weak riffles and exposed boulders. The Dolores runs chatoyant with silt. The rivers blend and flow toward the Colorado, ancient allies carving canyons.

At his favorite hole near the confluence a pickup advertises the virtues of panning for gold for money. Nearly every bit of what was once perceived to be the West is being sold, auctioned or hustled like a prized used car with one last shiny paint job before sawdust and STP in the tranny give up the reality of what actually remains.

The Jimmy drifts spitting rocks, dirt and pebbles. Shimmy, throttle and they roar away kicking up voluminous plumes of dust. Last winter he followed two bald eagles on this same dirt road, hoping to capture a photographic glimpse while there was enough left to capture. You never know. There's less each year.

An Edward Abbey quote he can't shake runs through his brain..."So get out there and hunt and fish and mess around with your friends, ramble out yonder and explore the forests, encounter the GRIZZ, climb the mountains, bag the peaks, run the rivers, breathe deep of that yet sweet and lucid air, sit quietly for awhile and contemplate the precious stillness, that lovely, mysterious and awesome space. Enjoy yourselves, keep your brain in your head and your head firmly attached to the body, this body alive and active, and I promise you this one sweet victory over our enemies, over those deskbound men with their hearts in a safe deposit box and their eyes hypnotized by desk calculators. I promise you this; you will outlive the bastards."

One with the rumble, he winds the four-bolt main 350 out, not a Ferrari alive can compete with the sweet roar comes out the broken tailpipe under the long bed's chassis.

With luck he'll make the magic hour when riffles glean the last of the setting sun and trout get crazy with longing for patterns they don't understand but always react to.

Mitigating

Rumor has it the ice is off Miramonte Reservoir. Fishermen are out in force and fish are being taken but not by me.

I drove the Miramonte Road several times in past weeks to see if it was open. The best time to fish Miramonte is when the ice recedes, temperature warms and fish are hungry enough to bite on damn near anything.

A week ago the road was dry and open, lake ice-bound except for long skinny stretches of open water. I swore I'd fish the following day but it snowed.

Last Friday I took my young pal Bubba fishing at Miramonte. We bought his license at Norwood Hardware along with salmon eggs, jars of garlic marshmallows in three screaming iridescent colors, took requisite rods, reels, hooks, sinkers, stuff for lunch, two chairs and the dog.

The wind over Miramonte blows with a sandpaper edge out of Utah. The kid is excited so we find a likely spot, haul the gear and set up. Other fools fishing in the wind huddle buttoned up. We rig, bait, cast and settle in against the wind, no way to tell if fish are biting since the waves tug on the line like a six-pounder with getaway in mind.

I hope the wind will subside and fishing improves. Not so. Wind cranks to gale force. You can't get out of your chair because it will tumble into the lake. Doesn't matter, we're having fun, the Cone is spectacular, wild geese honk, waves batter our lines. We hunker down.

Less hardy fools leave. My hands are numb from the wind chill. I ask my fishing partner if he's amenable to getting the hell out of there. He agrees. The heater in the truck works well enough to melt the soles right off your shoes. In a few minutes we're toasty on the back road through Dry Creek Basin blowing holes in realty signs along fence lines with a Ruger .44 Blackhawk in true western fashion.

Neighborhood of Strangers

We make for the river. Each time we pull up to a favorite spot somebody's already there. I don't want to lose my temper and spoil an otherwise fine day just because ten billion people in the world today all want something to do on a Sunday afternoon.

If we go to the most obvious spot we'll find space on the river to cast a few and enjoy the sunshine. I'm partially right. We find a spot, break out the rods and slide down the bank to the river. Downriver I catch a glance of five or six guys working their way up the middle of the hole we were going to fish. We exchange pleasantries, lie to each other as fishermen do. Bubba and I go upriver to a hole no fisherman occupies at this moment.

After working our way across the river we nymph and almost simultaneously get strikes. These fish are dancers, veritable walkers on water, miraculous, flashing rainbows in a wild display of liquid tap.

Fish are feisty this time of year with water temperature rising. River's clear in the morning, clouds with silt and snowmelt in afternoon. This is one of the finest times of the year to fish, before the snowmelt works the river into a rage, which lasts from June well into August.

Rose Morse from the Bedrock Store reports that the road to Buckeye Reservoir along Carpenter Ridge is open until you get to the shady spots in the pines and then it's soggy and boggy, always a good idea to bring your 4X when fishing Buckeye in spring.

There's Groundhog Reservoir on the back road to Dolores, which looks to be open and McFee Reservoir is certainly free of ice by now.

Still a bit early for Woods Lake but Trout Lake and Priest Lake may be opening up by now. Ridgway Reservoir had folks fishing along the south banks as I drove home from Montrose the other day so there's action from that direction. Columbine and Blue Lakes above Telluride won't be open for a few more months so put that on your fishing calendar for late July. The Dolores River is good fishing from below Lizard Head Pass all the way to Dolores and the West Fork towards Dunton. Leopard and Elk Creeks offer fine fishing when the rivers are crowded or murky and the beaver ponds along Ilium Creek are also productive for the adventurous angler.

It's getting warm enough for catfish fishing at lower elevations and both the lower San Miguel and Dolores Rivers offer opportunities and scenery. The confluence of the rivers between Uravan and Bedrock is a spectacular spot to fish or sit and enjoy. The catfishing is good all the way down to Gateway and beyond on the road to Grand Junction. You'd be hard pressed to find better scenery anywhere in the world.

Fishing for stripers, largemouth, smallmouth, walleye, pike, crappie, catfish at Lake Powell is mere hours away.

If you haven't got the fishing fever by now, you're beyond help and what you need to do is turn on the tube and find some orally administerable anesthetic to ease you through your lethargy. I'll be out fishing. Thanks for your cooperation.

We took home a mess of tail dancers for dinner and got back in time to read the Sunday papers. I could have lost it and stormed and fumed because there's too many people on my river but I stayed with it and turned the outrage around. I find, as I get older, that mitigating the attitude works.

Last One

Early September, low water, last river trip of the season. Fall weather promises relief from summer's scorchers. The vessel of choice for a low water trip a 15' baby blue fiberglass canoe I slid down a 40' embankment on Lizard Head Pass in a whiteout with a one-ton dually strapped to it.

Grocery shopping is minimal. A 15-footer doesn't allow for luxury. We'll fish for our dinner, pack plenty of water, camping and cooking gear. Fully loaded the blue canoe sports an inch and a half of freeboard.

We float beneath Interstate 70 and Denver and Rio Grande Western bridges, Art comfortable in the bow, me in the stern. Everyday worries disappear with the bridges when we round the first bend.

Crystal Geyser is four and a half miles downstream, an unplugged well unsuccessfully drilled for oil in 1936. The geyser blows approximately every 12 hours in a spectacular display with 60' spouts depending on the mood of the gases. Gases seeping into the well bore cause the geyser to erupt. 60 years of eruptions have created multi-layered flows down to the river in subtle varieties of cream, yellow, orange, rust, red and brown.

The unfortunate part of this otherwise delightful scene is a road leading to the spot. Partygoers leave their garbage and crap behind. I no longer stop for the geyser because the trash bums me out.

Landscape both sides of the river at this point is mild, slightly sloping with the San Rafael Swell visible downstream in the distance. We paddle, float, and make camp between Little Valley and Five Mile Wash.

Art is the best fly fisherman I know. On the Green River I had Art on my turf. I never saw anybody fly fishing for catfish in opaque, rich, silted water. I bring two Walmart sale special graphite composite rods. One rod has an old Zebco bait reel and the other an even older Mitchell spinning rig. Both reels are rigged with 6lb test Stren monofilament in case you hook a big one or get snagged on the bottom.

I show Art my favorite catfish fishing rig, a treble hook with an egg sinker about a foot and a half up the line with crimped split shot directly below the egg sinker. You wad up a clump of stink bait, which is made up of dog shit, coagulated blood and rotting limburger cheese on the treble hook, flang it into the river, let it bounce along the bottom in the current until it settles downstream and you settle in for a most satisfying and exciting tug on the line. Since catfish forage by scent rather than sight the tug shouldn't, with luck, take very long.

Art chooses the Mitchell, baits up and before long we have corn-mealed catfish filets deep-frying in virgin olive oil with fresh limes and salsa to add to the general goodness of life on the river.

I warn Art about the intensity of the sun on the river and tell him to bring along a wide-brimmed sombrero. He brings his fly fishing cap. Years of running rivers taught me a cowboy brim turned down makes wonderful shade against the sun's murderous rays. It also works as an excellent cooling rig when dipped into the water and placed on a bald head like mine. Art's nose gets redder each day but he won't swap hats.

No need to put up a tent, we lay Thermarests on ground cloths and lay out sleeping bags. The kitchen is simple, an Optimus propane stove, frying pan, coffee pot, spatula, two enameled blue metal plates, utensils and cups. We bring a fire pan to leave minimal trace of our having been there.

Coffee and fishing are first every morning. One of us gets coffee cooking while the other goes after catfish. We pick camp spots that look fishy. When the sun breaks over the canyon's rim we're packed and stroking downstream. We hunt for catfish and shade.

First shady spot looks fishy, a promising eddy or pool, we pull over and fish until the sun appears or the fish stop biting. Captive catfish are placed on a stringer and rigged off the gunwale as pets until lunch or dinner.

Art catches the first, last, biggest and most fish on our journey down Labyrinth Canyon. I'm not used to being whupped fishing by anybody but the fish, although I can't help but admire Art's style, determination and tenacity when it comes to figuring out technique.

He immediately goes for lighter rigs with smaller treble hooks using less bait. I wonder if that will work but my questions are answered when Art lands a catfish as long as my arm.

The river is extremely shallow that time of year. When we're grounded, which happens at least once a day, Art gets out of the bow and pulls, and I get out of the stern and push. We talk back and forth. Art can see better. Head down, I'm doing an imitation of a lineman blocking a sled.

One afternoon I don't get an answer from Art when I ask if he can make out an obvious channel. I look to see what's wrong. Art's gone. He comes up downriver sputtering and soaked. He stepped off the sandbar and discovered he couldn't touch bottom.

Art's face blisters, cracks and peels. I smear medicated goo on his nose and lips but each succeeding day he looks more like an escapee from a leper colony.

We have big fun with the catfish, live by the fire, talk with ravens cruising through the canyon, not a care besides finding a campsite and dinner, not another soul in sight.

We land at a hole with a huge rock at the head, a deep pool and a classic eddy. Art's gone like a shot, scrambles up the rock, casts a lump of stink bait to the center of the hole, tightens line, waits.

I hadn't even made the rock when quietly he says, "fish on," rod bent big time. Green River catfish are generally channel cats but occasionally bull catfish will take bait. Channel cats aren't very big but they are very tasty.

Art's catfish is as long as my arm, I know because I measure it, with a head the size of a volleyball, muddy black with whiskers long as my fingers, pissed off croaking "wrack, wrack, wrack." We hook him on the stringer, the stringer on the gunwale and fish the hole.

My two pound yellow catfish might be an occasion any other time but today it looks like a sardine.

We camp early, in the afternoon shade of a scrub oak grove on the downriver side of Bowknot Bend almost through Oak Bottom, with a sand beach and plenty of shade.

Art puts the big bull cat on top of a rock and whomps him upside the head. The catfish wriggles, mighty pissed off. Art whomps again and again and again. If this catfish is dead he doesn't show it or else doesn't care.

With professional aplomb, Art dispatches the big catfish with an entrenching tool, filets and releases him to the timeless cycles of life and death at the bottom of the river, nothing wasted.

Chicken in the Sink

Put the chicken in the sink to defrost before you leave home to fish a strange lake. That's an Art Rowell basic rule of thumb for fishing unfamiliar waters.

Art knows fishing. He shows up in Norwood last Friday night. I invited Art to fish San Miguel County. He finally takes me up on my offer.

Art arrives with a huge foil-covered pan of lasagna. Carla, Art's wife, knows men don't take care of business. She cooks lasagna so Art won't starve in two days of fishing. I'm glad to see the lasagna because Carla is an excellent cook and something of a fortune-teller also.

Early Sunday morning after coffee and breakfast, we pack our fly rods, waders and vests, off for the San Miguel. The river runs full, the color of thick coffee with skimmed milk, viscous with silt. We go on a tour of good holes from the Norwood Bridge to below Placerville. The river never lightens.

Looks like a still-water fishing day. The wind picks up. Miramonte is a possibility but minimal fun on a windy, warm day, especially with two anglers convinced a fly rod is the only way to go. We speed towards Buckeye Reservoir. Art lives in the Roaring Fork Valley, which is an OK place to live but can't hold a candle to the visual impact of the spectacular vistas we enjoy in the San Miguel Basin.

I pass the turnoff for Buckeye on my way to Moab, Salt Lake City, or the West Coast for a couple decades. This is an excellent opportunity for a recon mission to an area neither of us has been. Art's game and we're off.

Lone Cone is spectacular, San Juans brilliant to the east, Paradox and Disappointment valleys hazy to the west because of dry, hot, intense, moisture sucking winds which have blown steady for a few weeks. The LaSals appear behind a gauze curtain of dust blown off the desert floor. The wind is relentless, seeking out moisture wherever it can.

The topic of conversation inevitably turns to lack of moisture and how it's going to be a tough summer wherever we stop. Beginning of May and snow pack on the mountains is minimal with bare spots showing on ridges and peaks. Stock ponds are low with a stretch before summer's afternoon thunderstorms bring relief.

Rose Morse microwaves Polish sausages with Swiss cheese and mustard for sandwiches for our lunch. Paul Morse shows his newest wood creations in his shop in back. We get directions for the Buckeye road after hugs and goodbyes.

Carpenter Ridge Road to Buckeye climbs directly up steep red rock walls above Paradox Valley. Depending on the time of year, four-wheel drive is advisable. My old Toyota Land Cruiser huffs, puffs, chugs and clangs to the top. Once on top of the mesa, a refreshingly green ponderosa forest shades us on our way to the reservoir.

Glints of Buckeye's clear waters shimmer through the ponderosas. Soon the Toyota stands parked in the shade by the lakeshore and we don our waders. The peaks of the LaSals loom clearly behind us, no longer screened by curtained dust.

Fishing Buckeye is a new experience for both of us. We start with nymphs along the bottom, too windy to fish the surface with dry flies. Fish aren't rising that time of day anyway.

We flang Wolly Boogers, Callibetis nymphs, Beefus Scuds, Aspen Airhead Flies, Flashabuggers, all to no avail. We whip the waters of the tree-protected lagoon with orange and yellow floating lines. No dice, no fish, no nada. Finally I look into my fly box and find the ugliest and least likely nymph - a Green River Witch. The Witch is a black and chartreuse woven plastic concoction with a hairy tail that might, on a cloudy, dark night, win the ugly prize at a nymph convention. I rig and cast.

An immediate wham straightens line soon as I twitch the Witch in, a hellacious wham because I come up with nothing but empty leader. Either it was a great big fish, leader too light, or else my knot gave out. Art gets on my case because I'm using 7X tippet. The fish is gone along with my Green River Witch, the only one I had in my box because it was so ugly I thought nothing would go for it.

Neighborhood of Strangers

I have nymphs black and sparkly with drop heads and all sorts of concoctions but nothing approximating chartreuse. I look at Art's blue Frying Pan Anglers hat with chartreuse trim. Art won't part with the hat, not even for a shot at catching fish. I plead with him. Nothing doing, not even the braid along the brim. This is his lucky hat and he isn't going to let me have it.

We whip the water. I change tippets, nymphs and locations. Nothing doing. I try faking a nap to see if Art will fall asleep so I can get his hat. He doesn't fall for it. We hope the wind will fade in late afternoon, drive to the far side of the lake. About six o'clock we're worn down, decide to give it up and go home.

The road to the west of the lake proves smoother than the Carpenter Ridge Road. The ride to the valley floor is relaxed. No white-knuckle rock and roll on the way home. Around a bend coming out of the ponderosa one of the most incredible vistas I've seen in my life unfolds before us: the Paradox Valley looking directly east toward the San Juans with the Lone Cone tiny in proportion in the distance lit by the sun on its western descent behind the LaSals.

The drive to the Lone Cone Saloon is silent, cold beers in mind. We pound a couple and go home.

My sweetie has chicken sizzling over coals on the grill in the yard. Carla's lasagna is warming in the oven. Asparagus we picked in ditches east of Nucla is cooking with dill and butter. No fish but we share another excellent adventure, another a good day.

We're believers in the "It seemed like a good idea at the time" philosophy of life.

Next morning we drive Miramonte Road with ravens and buzzards flapping standstill in futile attempts to make headway. Still seems like a good idea.

The dust cloud behind us blows sideways, east. Undaunted, we drive on. The channel between the island and the north shore of the reservoir is calm in two to three second increments when we launch our flies, time for plan B.

Plan B has us driving in the direction of Beaver Park and hopefully Woods Lake down the back road past Little Cone. It's an incredibly good plan at its inception. We're out of the wind, the scenery can't be beat and not another car since Norwood and the dirt road is in great shape. Art comments on how quickly the snow pack is receding. Prospects of getting through to Woods Lake seem good.

Right after the road to Specie Mesa things get worse. We break through snow-covered turns until we arrive at a place where the snow is still several feet thick across the entire road an there's no proceeding, time for plan C.

For years I meandered all over the back roads of the county in a turquoise 57 Ford pickup in search of fishing, adventure, mushrooms and critters good to eat and easy to shoot. I vaguely remember a cattle track over Specie Mesa as we approach a Y in the road. Going back to Norwood the way we came is not an acceptable alternative. We take the track over Specie.

At first the going is easy and plan C realistic and workable. Then we encounter mud and lock the hubs. After mud comes winter-old, spring-heavy snow pack, time to shift into compound low. Luckily, we slide downhill through the worst of it, grind it out pedal-to-the-metal on uphill stretches, pound water and mud-filled holes airborne in the track, maintain momentum and direction. Mud splatter covers the windshield. I fixed the windshield squirters months ago in anticipation of just such a situation. The wipers and squirters work!

Art hangs on for dear life wondering why the hell he'd agreed to come along but he knows the answer already. A fishing trip with Uncle O is never boring. We don't always accomplish exactly what we set out to do but the view from the edge is always stimulating. Good thing adrenaline is legal.

We cruise downhill splattered in Specie Mesa mud, take a right turn at the river road for Placerville. The San Miguel runs high. I consider fishing Leopard Creek. The creek looks good but Art wants no part of any more bushwhacking. We make for Priest Lake below Trout Lake on Lizard Head Pass, pass Telluride and make a right towards Ophir. Wilson, Sunshine and Sheep Mountain open up before us like a geological symphony. The Ophir Wall is not chopped liver. I'm thankful and amazed to live in a place where beauty is so abundant and accessible. Art shows proper reverence repeating "Wow."

A turn or two through the Ophir Loops and we crank a left at Trout Lake, another for Priest Lake. The road ends in a few hundred yards blocked by snow. We hike in to the lake. At last, a body of windless water to fish and it's beautiful to boot. Gray-Hackled Yellowbodies always work for me at Priest Lake. Not today. No rises to the surface. We go below the surface with nymphs. Same result.

Could have been winterkill but I know better. It is the moon in booga-booga retrograde, wind in apocalyptic insanity, stars on vacation in South-Central with a Ripple hangover. The fishing is a bust. We cast and cast and come up with two questionable hits. Art has to be at work in the morning in Basalt and already it's late afternoon.

The Landcruiser backfires and dies a quarter mile down the road through Ilium. I check fuel, spark and timing. The moon in booga-booga laughs loon-like on the wind. I call my sweetie with a one word message - "Help!" She rescues us. I leave the Toyota where it died in the dirt.

Art makes it to work on time. The rig is towed, dead for the time being, distributor shaft twisted and broken, digested by the oil pump gears, also broken. There's lots of little chewed up pieces of metal in the oil pan. I bail and buy a beater GMC pickup with really cool yellow cab lights. She smokes some but I don't mind. She runs.

The Yo

The other day Peter Spencer said something that made me listen. He never names vehicles after women.

Historically, hurricanes were named after women. When I worked forests thinning trees with a Jonsereds chainsaw the crew named their saws after women. My saw was named Josef Stalin.

The Yo, as my not-so-trusty Land Cruiser is presently named, got its start last winter when my friend Maurice was broke and I was living at Steve Steed's place. If you've been up Steed's road you understand why I needed a 4X. Larry Kozey, Steed's closest neighbor, keeps the common road in outrageous disrepair to keep those who don't need to be there out. I agree. That's why I bought the Yo.

The deal for the Yo was made at the Lone Cone Saloon one Saturday afternoon. Maurice proposed I buy his '75 Land Cruiser station wagon. He made me a good deal and assured me the beast would indeed run with minor attention. I had a job and money so I went for it.

Paperwork on the Yo was nonexistent, nobody knew who owned what. With the aid of Doris Ruffe and Gay Cappis at the San Miguel County Clerk's office in Telluride, we got the paperwork under control. I hold title to the Yo. It took several months, the Colorado State Patrol, determination of the ladies at the County Clerk's office and tons of paperwork.

The Yo sat in Maurice's field for seven years, tires flat, interior ravaged by squirrels and mice, storage for stuff in various stages of decomposition. It was used to haul wood, took a week to clean up to where it could be worked on. We hauled the Yo out of the mud with a backhoe.

Neighborhood of Strangers

When the Yo turned over and ran we were ecstatic, like our lives would be nothing but pancakes with real maple syrup served by nude nubile maidens. A ham sandwich with mustard you make yourself is more like it.

The real work began once the Yo turned over. We replaced bearings, battery, fan belt and starter. Then came shocks, tires, wheel cylinders, plugs, wires, points, windshield, oil pan, turn signals, air filter, mirrors, fuel sending unit, headlight rings, carburetor rebuild kit, head gasket, valve guide seals and front end alignment.

Maurice hung in there with me through the process of getting the Yo roadworthy. He wasn't obligated to do any of it.

When the Yo died in front of the Lone Cone Saloon a couple weeks ago I was ready to give it up. Maurice assessed the problem in my front yard after we towed the Yo off the street. A new distributor cost about $300 with shipping and tax. We got the Yo running without replacing the engine. Empirical timing adjustment required a couple days.

The Yo gets me to good fishing spots and river trips, to work through snowstorms, not much to look at but great to drive. I helped bring this old tank back to life, got the heater and gas gauge to work. I'm not much of a mechanic so every small triumph is a big thing for me.

I agree with what Spencer said about naming cars after women. After 50 years of dealing with girlfriends, wives, PMS, foo-foo, friendship and immeasurable fun I'm convinced there's no need to name my Toyota after a woman. Yo will have to do.

The Green Hornet

My brand new Swedish razor-sharp ice auger has yet to bite on any local ice since both my driving rigs are down and I'm not likely to hike out to Miramonte Reservoir to sit on the ice waiting for a fish to bite my bait. They'll bite my "where the sun don't shine" before I'm likely to do that.

Both my trusty old Land Cruiser and the Olds decided to show their age and crapped out at the same time. The Land Cruiser died in front of the Lone Cone Saloon and the Olds died in Telluride in the ski area parking lot. Being stranded is not one of my favorite things to be and I was getting somewhat stressed until friends arrived with help, advice and solutions.

Billy Boyd helped me check out the Land Cruiser and we determined she was beyond immediate help in the street. We towed her to my house where she sits as a reminder that old junkers are exactly that. They require constant care and are more likely than not a pain in the ass, expensive to maintain and undependable. At this point I'm considering installing a Chevy 350 with a conversion kit but that's just dreaming since it's an expensive proposition.

Billy sensed that I was getting stressed out with the land Cruiser crapping out and reminded me that stress is no good for guys our age. We've been friends for close to 20 years so I didn't try to ease my stress factor by choking him. I smiled and thanked him instead.

The Olds died in the Telluride parking lot at the hands of my ex-girlfriend. I'll try my best attempt at acting like a gentleman and won't repeat what I said and how I feel.

Billy was right when he advised me to step away from the whole thing, let it pass and figure out a solution when calm returned.

Neighborhood of Strangers

Best of all was Peter Spencer who, when he heard of my dilemma, offered me his Green Hornet 72 Ford LTD to drive until I could resolve the situation. This is an awesome rig with a 390 cubic inch engine, body by bash with mange on the roof, green paint in several shades of fade and four studded snow tires.

She started right up after months of sitting behind The Post's offices. I'm in love.

After decades of driving some of the most awesome junk on the Great American Highway this is another installment of the rig of my dreams. My relationships with cars usually last longer than my relationships with women but then cars go at least 3,000 miles between oil changes and once they're paid for they stay that way.

I'll most likely have to take the rocker cover off the Yo, look at the valves and determine if one of them is stuck. Then I'll have to figure out what to do about it. Once I get that far I may as well take off the head and do a ring job since this monster eats oil like a defensive lineman eats Whoppers.

Maybe I'll trade in my junkers and get a good 4X rig that runs and make payments alongside all the fools that I've been quietly laughing at. It's the American Way. Nah.

The most amusing part of this whole deal is that I was going to write my column about the resurrection of the Yo, my not-so-trusty Toyota Land Cruiser and in a roundabout way I did. Only I didn't get to go fishing and the Eagles were losing 23-7 to the Cowboys in the third quarter when I turned the game off.

Some days it pays to cut your losses and look to a better day when the rig runs, the fish bite and everything's all right.

Lies

Near-truth and fish size stretching are accepted practice among fishermen of all nations, denominations, colors, styles and beliefs. It has been this way since the first man caught his first fish. He was willing to be neighborly and share a bite or two but wasn't willing to give away the secret of his new found wealth. He passed his skills and secrets to his progeny along with a penchant for stretching the truth. Fishing skill and truth stretching has since been passed down father to son, uncle to nephew and in rare cases father or mother to daughter over millennia.

The female of the species, in my experience, is somewhat reluctant to deal with threading worms, guts, rotting liver, etc. onto a fishhook. They're also reluctant to gut and clean fish although they gladly gather around the dinner table once the fish are cleaned, prepared and cooked. I found women to be somewhat prissy when it comes down to the blood and guts of fishing.

There have been women in my life who knew what to do when it came to fishing. They've been few and far between. For the most part I adhere to this philosophy when it comes to fishing: "Fish, cut bait or go home."

A woman friend from Moab amazed me on a river trip down the San Juan some years ago when she brought along a change of lingerie for every day on the river, complete with high heels. I never even thought about applying the "Fish, cut bait or go home" philosophy with her. I did manage to catch one six-pound catfish before we took out at Clay Hills Crossing. I may be stretching the truth about that catfish since it's been a while. Might be that fish was actually ten pounds.

Truth stretching, believe it or not, is practiced right here in San Miguel County. I'm not talking about unscrupulous lawyers, realtors, developers, politicians, advertising types, car salesmen or insurance salesmen but about fishermen. On any given day at the Lone Cone Saloon or the Hitchin' Post you'll see guys sitting on bar stools in the middle of the afternoon animatedly talking and gesturing with their hands. Once the hands come out in a gesture of measure and the measure grows along with the story you can rest assured that the fish the guy is describing isn't the only whopper involved. The size of fish caught grows in direct proportion to how long ago that fish was caught and how many beers the teller is into.

The difference between truth stretching among unscrupulous types and fishermen is that fishermen do it for the pure joy of putting one over on you and getting you to bite just like the fish they caught. Their version of truth stretching is based in historically approved distortion of fact to disguise something they need to protect like their pride, a secret hole, special bait or an especially effective technique. The rest lie for money. There's a huge difference in the artful aspects of somebody telling you a story for fun and somebody trying to get their sleazy fingers in your wallet.

What it boils down to is every true fisherman has his own way to fish. Fishing is an intimate experience and nobody's business but your own. If somebody asks you how the fishing is you'll most likely say it's slow or it stinks even though you've got a stringer full. People who beg for information deserve what they get until they figure out what they need to know. Once they get it, they'll be doing it too.

If the truth is to be taken with a grain of salt, fishing stories and advice should be very salty indeed. There's a handful of friends I'd tell what's actually working on a particular day on particular fish. There rest are on your own. I'm certain the reverse is true, salty stuff, this fishing.

Beware fishing shows on the tube especially. Fishing is the #1 sports business in the U.S. and these guys are out to sell you a bill of goods. If you're an actual fisherman you know that every fishing day isn't a day you limit out and there's days when you get totally skunked. The hotshots on TV'll have you believing that they kick ass on the fish every time out. Not so. What I think they do is have a guy in a scuba outfit with a tank full of fish they hook on every time the director feels it's necessary for the pro to hook into a trophy bass, salmon or whatever. All you need to be a TV fisherman is the ability to say "Nahs fish, nahs fish, y'all." Think about it.

When I'm out fishing I'm protective about what I'm catching, how much or if any at all and with what. My daddy never fished, didn't like it. He didn't like to eat fish either. What I learned about fishing I learned from truth stretchers and hardcore fishing types. What I learned is that you have to figure it out yourself unless you've got a benevolent grandpa who doesn't care if you catch more fish than he does.

Another day some years ago with a different friend on a river trip down the Green River, we were sitting on shady flat rock having leftover fried catfish filet sandwiches and cold beer for lunch. Around the bend comes a guy with his girlfriend in a blue canoe trailing an inflated green plastic alligator. He asks what we're having for lunch. We tell him. He asks if the fishing's any good. I reply that it's rotten despite the fact that I've got a stringer full from that morning. I don't know why I did that. I suppose it was reflex.

"That's great," the guy in the blue canoe says, "we're having yummy noodles."

What I have learned since I figured out that fishing's fun is you ain't catching diddly unless you've got a bait in the water. If it doesn't work, change it. You'll figure it out if you haven't already.

71

Different

The San Miguel is murky from a glance off the first hairpin down Norwood Hill. Fishing minimal, I toe the Olds past the posted limit. With luck the State Patrol are on some other stretch of road today.

I check my favorite fishing spots at speed, riffles and pools gain volume the color of weak coffee spiked with skim milk. The Olds nudges past the limit, funky smooth rhythm and blues blowing through familiar curves, not a cop in sight.

At Leopard Creek the silt slows to light murky green, takes to Sawpit to slow down to consider fishing. A ride along the San Miguel is a song you can't get out of your head, once it gets rolling no way to stop it. I flang nymphs and flies but nary a nibble, no fooling the trout today. Frankly, my dear, they don't give a damn.

I decide to fish for a deal in Telluride. It's off-season and the possibilities are good. Shoes I bought at the KOTO ski swap saw me through winter but it's time for a new pair of kicks. I have a job and plastic fantastic to spread around.

After tourists go back where they came from we get our old town, mountains and what's left of collective sanity for a respite before the next onslaught. Off-season never lasts long enough for me. A Main Street cruise yields yupster and hipster nonsense wear. I chart a course for Paragon Sports.

"I won't sell these to ya," the youngster in charge says, "but I'll let ya buy 'em."

I come in looking for a deal, try trail running gel specials on sale. I'm not likely to run because I'm too old and it doesn't agree with my titanium hip.

"What you need are bombproof Nikes," the kid says. He explains why I should have shoes not on sale. I don't care. They fit. The kid is right, knows his stuff. There's hope for Telluride. Last time I bought a pair of shoes fit this well was in a high dollar shop in D.C. when a pair of handmade English shoes for $300 were no big deal

I give the kid plastic, walk out with a big smile. Feels so good I take my old kicks to the free box. A town with a free box can't be all bad. Years ago I'd take my discard kicks to a favorite fishing hole or to a spot where the view adds a million acres to my outlook on life.

I sit in the Sheridan Bar window with a draw. Old friends appear. I could have sworn it was fifteen years ago. Off-season clears the air enough to pick out old timers, spot the ghosts along streets and alleys. I'm glad to see'em all, comfortable in my bombproof kicks.

I didn't catch a fish but hooked a hell of a deal, shared good times with old friends and saw a town I had given up for lost. There's fishing days don't turn out like I plan because they turn out better.

Green

A cure for doldrums caused by several weeks of being cooped up, laid up and fed up, comes to me while recuperating from a hip replacement operation: a river trip down Labyrinth Canyon; enough crutches and canes!

I reach Mike Boren in Abilene and propose an expedition starting April Fools Day, spiritual birthday of artists and fools. Mike, a solid road pal for 20 years, agrees.

We meet in Moab, put in at Green River State Park. Crystal Geyser, five miles from the put-in erupts as we round the bend. The geyser erupts periodically due to gases, which seep into an unplugged oil well drilled in 1936. It blows 50 to 60 feet high as we float by on a bed of early spring silt. We take it as a good omen.

We camp early, a few miles downriver. I fish for the delicious channel catsfish, which inhabit the Green. Mike facilitates whatever new spiritual direction he's entertaining at the moment whether it comes out of a bottle or a left-handed hand rolled.

"I'm like an orangutan trying to fuck a football when it comes to catching fish," Mike says. We'd been on expeditions on three continents. He is an ape when it comes to fishing.

A ferocious thunderstorm blows my fishing plans to hell that evening. Mike and I swap lies and theories until the stars come out and the fire in front of our tent turns to ash and coals.

We break camp and immediately look for shade, my formula for a successful river trip. Soon as we find shade, we tie up at an available fishing hole, get a bait in the water and kick back until the first electric tug. As sun climbs and shade recedes, we hook our catfish on a stringer as temporary pets and row down river. By lunch we have enough cats on our stringer for a delicious meal.

Take the first catfish off the stringer. Don't get punctured by dorsal or pectoral fins, it really hurts. Take pliers and when the cat opens his mouth, grab a solid hold, whomp him upside the head like you really mean it. Take your knife, make an incision around and forward of the dorsal fin. While holding your catfish with the pliers in his mouth take another pair of pliers and peel his skin off. This may be tough for some of our squeamish readers because catfish talk. They say "Wrack, wrack, wrack," until you whomp 'em upside the head. Then they don't say it anymore.

Flop him sideways on a board when he's skinless and filet the yummy sucker, then flang the carcass in the river for his little friends to eat. This is how filet and release conservation was born. Catfish eat anything and they're not prejudiced.

Wash filets off in the river and plop into a handy ziplock. When the bag is full, open your cooler and ice down the filets.

If you can't wait for dinner set up the stove, pour enough virgin olive oil to fry well in your skillet and light the flame. The oil has to be hot, hot, hot. Take the filets, cut them into two to three inch sections and plop them in another ziplock with Uncle O's Custom Fishfry Zango in it. My favorite recipe for catfish is a mixture of cornmeal and cajun spice, just enough spice to take the yellow off the cornmeal and put some zango in your batter. When the fish are covered put them in the olive oil and fry until they're golden crispy and ready for the fresh lime you remembered to pack this trip.

Lay the fish out on a newspaper, to soak up excess oil, squeeze the lime on and it's time to chow down. Sometimes I bring salsa and hot sauce for extra zango. A cold beer is nice as long as the ice lasts. There's an art to packing ice for river trips.

If you pay attention to shade and fishing you'll be incredibly comfortable, productively occupied and never have to dig into your stash of store-bought food your entire trip except for the cookies, which go fast when the munchies hit.

Mike's major contribution on the trip is burning trash at the end of the day, keeps the flies down in the raft.

Mike stays up late, feeds the fire, watches stars, burns trash and drinks whiskey. Next day he has a new batch of theories to spout and endless stories about women to spin. Silence for Mike is a frightening state of affairs. Good thing he's a crafty storyteller who doesn't repeat himself much.

The water heals.

Gray

The fishing gear is laid out on the couch before the last play of the game when Philly ices the victory over Dallas. The Eagles' win is awesome, a linebacker interception in the end zone, lateraled to a speed-burning defensive back for a 104-yard touchdown: Philadelphia 31, Dallas 21. The Cowboys were about to score when fate and a good linebacker stepped in.

A good day to watch football, Sunday is slushy, slick, gray. No need to go outside since there's entertainment enough on the tube with the best game of the year. During the third quarter I decide I'd rather go outside and play. When the barometer drops, the hunger factor in fish increases.

Huge flakes of sloppy snow pelt the windows. I get off the couch, gather chest waders, felt-soled lace ups, fishing vest and rod case. I lay the gear out on the couch and settle in to watch the Cowboys pull it off once more in Irving, Texas. When Philly scores I holler and jump for joy. I'm not a Dallas fan.

When Fox Network rolls and re-rolls the lateral and touchdown I don fishing gear, secure the fishing is going to be spectacular today. I'm not so sure it would be any good if you're a Cowboy fan. You've got to have a feeling for these things. I turn the TV off.

When weather is this crummy most fair-weather fishermen, esoteric types who need permission from the old lady to go out to torture and release fish, then come home for a burger, steak or veal picatta, most likely are watching PBS, cooking shows or playing patty cakes with the liberated wife, provided she doesn't have a headache.

No traffic, Norwood Hill is littered with rocks. Low clouds and fog obscure the slippery roadway. I waited all fall for a day like this when I can have at least a small portion of the river to myself. I never shared my women, well, maybe once or twice. I certainly don't intend to share my river.

The magic of solitude on a rainy, snowy day on the San Miguel is all-consuming, as heavy flakes pelt and penetrate whatever cap and foul weather gear you're wearing, as the clear, dark flow slips around your legs, waist, chest and you can barely see beyond where the line plays out and drops the Stonefly nymph into the pool ahead, swirling softly before the backdrop of pale clutter against the wintry evening sky.

The strike indicator disappears below the surface of the current and you tug back quickly on the rod, gathering line, feeling for a strike. FISH ON! First downstream, then up, then deep, tip up, I work the fish to the bank. A pan-sized rainbow trout slides into the pocket in back of my vest. I feel along the bottom for firm footing, look upriver for another likely spot a fish would hang looking for an easy meal on a lovely gray day like this. Another cast, another strike.

Four keepers and I'm soaked, satisfied and ready for another hole. I'll warm up and dry out in the truck to give it one more try.

Three curves down the road, a rockslide litters the highway, I turn around and go home.

Friends arrive for dinner. They bring wine. We have trout and rice for dinner. They must have shown themselves out. I fall asleep in front of the TV, another ballgame on.

Ice

The shapes, forms, billows and colors the river assumes in winter are spectacular if you're into photography. Fishing the river is out of the question.

Sunday a week ago I drive to Miramonte reservoir with left-over fishing holes in the ice like frozen-over craters. The ice sings eerie Star-Trek-like songs of otherworldly whales. If you've been on the ice you know what I mean. If you haven't, you should go. The ice holds without cracking. I gingerly walk around inspecting augured ice scars.

Convinced ice fishing is a great idea, I dig spinning rods out of storage, find years-old salmon eggs, promise myself to buy canned corn at the Norwood market. I drive to Montrose and buy a Swedish ice auger, da kine. I'm rigged for ice fishing but contract a case of the crud, which postpones everything until after Christmas.

I recall white-knuckle drives through the Ophir Loops with Mike Baer, chopping at the hole in the ice with a heavy-duty digging bar left over from the heyday of mining in Telluride. First time I dig the hole, I send the bar to the bottom with the final stroke, have to finish with a high-lift jack careful not to send the jack to the bottom too. I'm an ice-fishing veteran, you see.

Sunny days we stand around and hardly ever catch fish. If it storms, blows, and raises hell we limit out and crawl back to the truck in a blizzard, ass-deep in crusted snow, facing the Ophir Loops, Lawson Hill and Keystone on the way home.

I never understood how two guys could be ice fishing a couple feet apart and one guy catches fish while the other stands sour-pussed with nothing showing except a degenerating attitude. We change holes and it makes no difference. Same bait, same depth, same hole, same result. It can drive a guy crazy.

Neighborhood of Strangers

After skating through my memories I'm not about to head out in a snowstorm to test out my razor-sharp Swedish ice auger.

A toasty fire crackles in the wood stove, there's hot coffee with dark rum, the playoffs are on the tube and Philadelphia kicks the living shit out of Detroit in the wildcard game. I'm an Eagles fan for four decades with very little to cheer about, ecstatic today with 51-7 score before the Eagles bring second and third stringers in.

I'll go ice fishing first sunny day Philly's not playing. Ice'll be here all winter.

Auger

Finally, after depleting my excuses bag, I went ice fishing at Miramonte Reservoir last Friday.

It was an exquisite day, nearly sultry for January. The gear was laid out—fishing poles and reels, bait, split shot, hooks, a director's chair and a bright blue Mora razor-sharp Swedish ice auger.

The road to Miramonte was absolutely no hassle since it hasn't snowed any appreciable amount this winter. When I arrived at the reservoir I discovered there were half a dozen ice fishermen with the same idea. There was plenty of room to fish.

At first I had to consider where to cut my hole in the ice. Everything I'd heard from ice fishermen so far this winter dictated that I head to the vicinity of the dam and let the Mora bite the ice. That's exactly what I did.

The Mora is an awesome tool, precise, easy to handle, and in a matter of minutes I'd augured through seven or eight inches of ice, cleared out the slush and, after setting up the director's chair and baiting up sent my hook, bait, line and sinker hopefully towards the bottom of the lake.

Seconds after the rig touched bottom I brought it up a few feet with anticipation of at least a light tug on the line.

Daisy, my dog, was laid out on the snow beside me, sunning like the star attraction she knows she is. I scratched her rump, told her I was about to deplete the lake of its largest trout, adjusted my Bolles and lifted my face to the sun to enjoy the rays, with a finger on the line in case I got an opportunity to make good on my boast to the dog.

A half hour later I checked the bait. Nothing had bothered it. I sent it back down and went through the same drill, only raising the rig a few feet every ten minutes to determine at what depth the fish were indeed feeding. They weren't.

This is usually the time to change the bait. I did, still no results.

I changed it once again and sent it down once again to some indeterminate depth and settled in, determined to not get skunked.

The sun and views were pleasant enough to occupy my interest and soon enough I was dozing off, enjoying reveries which cannot be detailed in earnest in this column because we are, after all, a family newspaper.

I woke to find Daisy was in the process of wandering off looking for something fun to do. I whistled her back, scratched her tummy and checked the bait again. Nothing doing.

We were into our second hour of nothing doing by then and I was beginning to think about doing something else. None of the ice fishermen around me were catching anything besides rays either.

Remembering back to years ago when I was younger and more easily amused, it occurred to me that the best times to get substantial results ice fishing were during snowstorms. On nice days you get bupkis and a tan. The prospect of staying in my director's chair until a snowstorm hit didn't appeal to me. Neither did getting out into a snowstorm to freeze my butt off hoping for the fish to change their minds.

The prospect of bringing friends along, some beer or maybe margaritas and something else to munch on besides visions of ex-lovers occurred to me as a swell way to pass the day at Miramonte getting sunstroke in mid–winter. Unfortunately I didn't think of this before I left home that afternoon. Most of my friends were working, as was I.

Daisy was happy because there was something new to do. I was happy because I didn't have to sit in the director's chair directing nothing, pretending that I actually gave a damn.

As we drove off I looked with puzzlement at the ice fishermen still there. It was beyond me why they sat there unless they know something I don't but it'll have to remain a mystery because I don't want to know.

The two guys to my right kept drilling holes like that was going to change their luck. Perhaps those two were miners. They were out to the middle of the lake by the time I left.

The two guys to my left were stoic, taking time only to go pee in the bushes.

The voices of laughing, playing kids over the hill indicated somebody out here was having fun and I'm sure the kids weren't fishing.

Despite rumors that there have been some lunkers taken at Miramonte this winter I was certain I'd made the right decision. Besides, the top of my head had started to get sunburned. There was rum at home and work to do and I had done enough research for one day.

Daisy licked my ear and wagged her tail as we drove off. I knew we were on the right track going home.

Crawdads

The Rocky Mountain critter that's easiest to catch and most delicious to eat is the crayfish, the crawdad, the mudbug. The crayfish is actually a freshwater crustacean of the tribe Astacura, resembling the lobster but much smaller.

The crayfish resembles lobster in more than just looks. Local crawdads are high-elevation miniature versions of saltwater crustaceans every bit as delectable as their ocean-going cousins.

This time of year crawdads become more active with warming weather. The season usually lasts from mid-June to mid-September. I've noticed plenty of crawdads in recent fishing forays. It should be a great year for both novice and expert alike.

Some bait fishermen consider crawdads a nuisance. Crawdads tug at and steal their bait. I'm thankful for these fishermen because that leaves more crawdads for true epicureal enthusiasts.

It doesn't take a Range Rover, hundreds of dollars worth of equipment or years of entomological or ichthyological expertise to catch a crawdad. What a beginner needs is bait, string, a long handled net, a bucket, and patience. Anybody with a fishing license can do it. Miramonte Reservoir is an excellent place for crawdads. Once you're better at catching crawdads you'll want to upgrade your equipment.

Best to use bait that will last because crawdads attack in numbers and tear bait up with their claws. Chicken necks, for instance, work well. They work even better if you let'em sit in the sun so they're good and stinky. Tie the chicken neck or whatever you decide to use for bait to the end of a string and flang that sucker into the water. Let it settle to the bottom and wait. Drink beer while you wait, smooch with your toots, take a walk or rig up more. A dozen or more baits in the water at the same time make for a lively afternoon, evening or night.

While I gather crawdads from one, the rest get loaded up. I move from one to another and don't need to come up with other stuff to do.

Night is best for crawdad hunting, cooler, the wind usually dies down and you can get a fire going to boil water for the crawdad pot. Check the local regs first and find out if there's a burning ban before you light up. Crawdaddys are tough critters and will last until you get home. A good idea for the neophyte is to go crawdaddying in daylight until you get the hang and feel of it down.

Once you've got a bunch on your bait, hunker down at the edge of the water, grab hold of the string and pull the string in softly, lightly so as not to scare the greedy little critters off your bait. Have your long-handled net handy when the crawdads are within reach, slip the net under them and net them. A few may get away but don't fret, crawdads have a very short memory and they'll be back as soon as you flang your bait back in the water.

This is where the bucket comes in. A plastic 5-gallon bucket of the restaurant variety works very well. Dump the crawdads into the bucket. Don't sit on the bucket while crawdads are in it because they'll get'cha. Be careful. They'll nail you with their claws if you're not quick and handy. It hurts. Take my word for it.

Crawdads take a defensive stance with claws up when they're threatened. If you've managed to get them out of the lake and are planning to dump them in a pot of boiling water be careful because they have every right to feel defensive. Don't get discouraged. It's well worth the effort. No pain, no gain.

Keep checking baits and filling up the bucket. Once the bucket is full you can either dump your catch into a large pot of boiling water which you've been heating over your fire or else pack'em up in the back of your pickup and go home. If you're a rookie you may want to try the next part at home to start with.

Once you're home get water boiling in a large pot. Bring the crawdads in to the house but watch out for escapees. You know why.

If you can wait for the feast overnight, prepare buckets with salt water and put the crawdads in them to purge crustaceans of the green-black poop in the vein that runs along their tail. If you can't wait then plop'em into the boiling water after you've spiced it up. You can clean the poop out with a thumbnail if you're squeamish. Or else you can just blow it off and get down.

What you need in the water is Zatarains Crab Boil, or Bay Seasoning or a concoction of cayenne, salt, Worcestershire sauce combined with sliced lemon, potatoes and corn. Experiment to suit your own taste.

Let the crawdads boil until they turn a bright orange-red, lift'em out of the boil and dump'em out on the table, which you've covered in newspaper. Facilitates cleanup later on.

I like to dip them in a couple different sauces. Drawn butter with mashed garlic is a favorite, as is a sweet, tangy red sauce with peppers and onions. You'll need a fresh loaf of French bread, cold beer or white wine to drink.

Once the boiled crawdads are on the table pick one up, tear it in half, peel the tail and have at it. Hardcore crawdad enthusiasts suck the juice out of the head. This is accepted practice in the South but since we're in Southwestern Colorado head sucking is optional.

Not so bad once you get used to the idea.

Fourth

Fishing gear is carefully and neatly stashed in the black box behind the cab. I'm trying my best to keep the pedal from the metal as I make my escape from the chaos of Colorado Avenue in Telluride.

A holiday weekend and the local constabulary are primed for any imaginable variety of outlaw, no time to get pulled over for doing 17MPH in a 15MPH zone. Such a shame what money and the people who enforce it have done to what used to be a civilized place to live.

During breakfast at Karen's I found about Roudy being made, by one muscle-brained female Telluride cop, to walk rather than ride his horse in the parade. This was done at the behest of one of Telluride's latter day image mongers, the wife of the owner of the ski area. Roudy loaded is far better on his horse than most riders are sober. And he's funny.

Keith LaQuey wasn't allowed to have a Harley Davidson escort in the parade because Harleys apparently don't fit the Telluride image. This is the Fourth of July and Harleys are right up there with mother-hood, apple pie and the Stars and Stripes. Not in Telluride.

I went to the parade in Nucla with real, live, down home Americans. No image problems here. Nucla loves the rumble of Harleys.

To hell with Telluride's image mongers, crowds, chaos and yup-pie bullshit. I'm on my way out of town looking for a place to fish.

At the Norwood Bridge I rumble along with the reverb of my GMC's rebuilt 350. The top of Norwood Hill always has a calming effect on me. I decide to try Miramonte Reservoir. Long before the end of the pavement I turn around. There's major traffic on Miramonte Road. At this point I'm in no mood to fish but I do want to find some peace and quiet without locking the doors and turning off the phone at home.

Neighborhood of Strangers

I steer the Jimmy for Paradox Valley. The afternoon is cloudy, promising some relief on the ride to Moab. The windows of the truck are down, the stereo is off and I'm listening to sweet roar of the new engine, pedal not quite to the metal.

At the Colorado State Highway 90 turnoff to LaSal I get the bright idea to go catfishing at one of my favorite spots at the confluence of the San Miguel and Dolores rivers down below Uravan. It's a great ride down the dirt road but there's already somebody at my favorite spot when I arrive. Some days you've got to laugh to keep from crying. The only fishing I'll do today is stretching the limits of believable stories with pals over beers at the Rio in Moab.

Even the Bedrock Store has got a power of parked cars outside as I blow by. It's hard to visit when it's busy.

At the top of the switchbacks before LaSal I stop to fill up a water bottle from the spring that flows off the side of the road. I stick my head under the cold, spring water flow in a ritual wake-up.

Moab is a visit with river running friends getting ready for a huge yard sale the following day. I get first crack at the good stuff and find an old red Schwinn bicycle with wide handlebars, balloon tires and a comfy sprung seat. There's no question the bike is going home with me. I load it in the truck along with extra tubes, tires, a wooden-handled stainless spatula, a whisk and a weathered old Louisville Slugger. The whole danged deal costs me $30 and there's money enough left for beers at the Rio.

Out of the oppressive heat of the afternoon I meet more old pals at the Rio on a Friday after work. We swap a few lies, drink a few beers and stretch a few stories.

I consider staying overnight but the heat is more than I'm willing to take. I'm off for Norwood and the cool breezes of Colorado night at home, after goodbyes.

Rains most of the way home. At the end of Paradox Valley the sky to the north lights up iridescent creamsicle pink with cobalt clouds below and lavender-streaked bright blue above as lighting flashes horizontal strikes above the red rock ridgeline.

The windshield wipers squeak as I make the turn for home. The rain is good, so is the day and soon my favorite spots will once again belong to me. Some days you do the best with what you've got and that's enough.

Old Eyes

"Goddamn these old eyes," he mutters over and over. He lost his best #16 Royal Wulff, right along with the entire 6X tippet first cast.

An unmistakable rise shows along the cut bank where the river makes a turn after the shallows has his attention, a big, sweeping lefthander of a crushing turn with snowmelt-smoothed rock sculpted eddies and swirling breaks for fish to feed in.

Takes a while for him to work his way down the center of the river where rocks obstruct the soft flow in beshadowed evening shallows. The neoprene and steel knee brace holds solid, providing him with an aging man's hopeful sense of security. The knee will take no more operations, sounds like a garbage can full of spare parts, worn out in the exuberance of his youth.

Finally, he has to take his time, unable to power over or through whatever's in his way. Balance is precarious but familiar. Worn felt soles of his outdated rubber waders feel for secure footing in the light play of the current and arrhythmic patterns of the river's bed.

He unhooks the #16 Royal Wulff he so carefully tied onto the 6X tippet at home from the ring on the split bamboo rod. Two false casts and the fly touches down in the riffles above the chute where the fish feed between rocks. The white-winged imitation floats gingerly on riffle tips. He feels the jolt as a trout furiously slams the fly, then nothing but slack line. The fly and tippet are snapped off, embedded in the trout's jaw.

He curses sullenly as he ties another tippet on in the twilight. No more small Royal Wulffs in his selection. He can't see well enough to tie another on anyway. When the fly is far enough away so he can see it, the hole in the shank, along with the tippet become a blur.

"The hell with this," he whispers to nobody but himself, the river and the fading light. There is another Royal Wulff in the flybox, a

#12, big enough to see. With luck he clinches the knot, ginks the Royal Wulff and casts again to the same spot. Nothing doing, that fish is long gone but others rise in the pool around him.

Cast after cast he feels jolts, hooks fish. Some shake the hook off with explosive tail dancing routines on the river's scarlet and orange-tinged wavy molten gold surface. Others he nets and lets go, plenty of time to catch some for dinner.

Nearly dark when he looks upriver and works his way to the north bank. He moves slowly, feeling his way, teetering as his waders slip on a mossy rock, one more pool before he's to the gravel road where the truck is parked.

He casts. Another hit, another dance of tortured leaps and insane gyrations. He nets the fish and whomps it flat in one smooth motion. He slips the fish in a front pocket of his vest. One more for dinner and it's time to climb out and hike up to the truck.

The final vestiges of sunset glow in the distance along the deepening purple sky behind the LaSal Mountains to the west as he crests Norwood Hill.

The blackened cast iron skillet sizzles with the slap of salt and pepper-spiced gutted trout. A cloud of smoke rises as fish curl in the pan. The smell of trout frying fills the room. The aroma of fresh-cut lime quarters awaits.

His creased, weather-furrowed face breaks into a smile, smoothing years off in a chuckle.

"Goddamn these old, decrepit eyes," he laughs.

Rocky Mountain Oysters

A layer of lush green grass with elongated stretches of millions of tiny deep lavender blooms lines Colorado State Highway 90 on either side of the entrance to Paradox Valley a few miles east of Bedrock.

The snowcaps of Tukhanikavits, patriarch of the LaSal range, loom massive over the red rock walls containing the valley. A corral with a dust cloud from hundreds of bellowing cattle appears off a dirt road to the left.

Tremulous calves dart in and out of the huddled herd to escape the heeling of mounted cowboys intent on their work. No contest, hooves of bawling calves are snapped tight by precisely flung lariats and dragged to staked ropes softened by inner tubes. The calves are tied, wrestled, dumped, stretched by the lariat firm to the saddle horn.

The cowponies move with the ease and audacity of a Super Bowl running back. Quick and decisive, they cut off escape routes, sense the riders' directions, wheel and turn, back up keeping tension on the rope perfectly tight - horse and rider fluid as one.

Cowboys and cowgirls clip ears, slit and remove testicles, inoculate, brand, sear horn remnants fast as they can, get calves on their feet and back with the herd.

The process takes timing, cooperation, and the precision of a team of skilled professionals. These cowboys follow traditions of southwestern cattlemen who've worked wild ranges for over a hundred years.

"We're keeping the art of being a cowboy alive," says Dan Moyer, cow boss, bloody hands sharpening his folding knife on a whetstone after he deposits a pair of Rocky Mountain oysters, fresh calf testicles, in a plastic bucket specifically reserved for this purpose.

"I'm romancing the past as long as I can, " Moyer explains,

"other ranchers do it the farmer way with steel tables. We do it the old way, the way cowboys did it back when. The people working here are real cowboy ranchers helping each other."

The red dirt of Paradox Valley and calf excrement soil the leather and denim of branders, cowhand shins bruised by explosive calf hooves. Acrid smells of calf hair and hide searing mix with dust and fill the air. Calves scamper away like nothing actually changed.

Propane-fed flames heat horn irons, branding irons, beavertails. Fresh "oysters" cook on steel drums containing the flames. Workers partake of the feast, comes with the territory, and with ceremony regard for the past and deep-seated cowboy traditions.

Blackened fresh "oysters" are good. Some hot sauce I might have had more.

1995-1996
FEATURES, INTERVIEWS
& CHARACTERS

Silverhawk Cowboss

He reveres and romances the past, lives and works in the present and expresses concern for an uncertain future for the working cowboy tradition.

Dan Moyer is cow boss of the Silverhawk Ranch in Nucla, Colorado. He's responsible for the day-to-day operation of a working cattle ranch.

Moyer comes from homesteader stock, grew up in the Rifle/Meeker area and has been around cattle and cowboys most of his life. He also worked as a "connector," building skyscrapers all over the United States and South Africa, working in the air connecting girders. He's an outfitter of considerable renown, Colorado State 1,000-yard shooting champion, a horse trainer and trader, and craftsman of traditional cowboy horse bits.

Tradition plays a large part in Moyer's life. He has put considerable effort into researching and documenting his family history.

Dan's great-great grandfather was from Indiana, killed in the Civil War. His great-great grandmother married a Dunkard preacher. Moyer's great-grandfather, who was 16 at the time, couldn't stand the preacher and ran off to St. Louis, Missouri, where he went to work for a rancher.

The rancher also had a freighting business and took Dan's great-grandpa under his wing. He found the boy was good with horses, gentle, had a way with them. Moyer's great-grandpa learned the freighting business and became a teamster.

The rancher bought a bunch of cattle in Old Mexico but unfortunately they had hoof and mouth disease. He didn't know that. When he drove the cattle up they spread the disease to all his neighbors. He wound up having to destroy all his cows, pay reparations to his neighbors. The rancher knew it was going to break him, knew he couldn't do much for great-grandpa but gave him a team of his choice and a freighter wagon.

Great-grandpa left and wound up in Leadville, Colorado, during the silver boom. He knew Wild Bill Hickock, who was also a freighter, but didn't like him.

Great-grandpa married a woman named Harmon and after the silver boom they went to Antlers, Colorado, and kept on freighting. Antlers was a stage stop between Rifle and Silt. At that time Rifle had one of the largest stockyards in the country. Dan Moyer played in that stockyard as a kid.

The grandfather's two older sisters, Nellie and Carrie, raised him because his dad was always on the road, like a long haul trucker is today. An old mountain man named Oscar Dudley, who knew Jim Bridger, taught Dan's grandpa how to trap and shoot. Moyer's family still has the rifle that the town of Rifle was named after. Oscar Dudley gave that rifle to Dan's grandfather.

By the time Dan was fifteen he was making a living on his own, cowboying, working on a ranch for an old woman who had outlived her husband by 20 years. Everything on the ranch was done the traditional way, no modern equipment, using teams to feed.

Dan and his dad weren't getting along at the time and that's how Dan got to go to work for the old woman. Dan's older brother Tom, who was 18, got into the ironworkers apprenticeship program, was making a lot of money, driving a brand-new pickup. Dan was working as a cowboy making dirt wages.

Dan gave up cowboying and went into the apprenticeship program for three years. He became a connector, liked to work in the air, built up a reputation and worked connecting all the highest buildings in Denver.

In 1983 he was one of seven ironworkers picked to go to Johannesburg, South Africa. Dan worked in New York, New Jersey, Los Angeles, Alaska, Louisiana. He worked connecting the power plant in Nucla.

For 13 years Dan cowboyed part of the year and worked iron the remainder. When his daughters were old enough to start school, Dan realized he'd have to find a place, which would be a good home for them. He wanted his kids to be able to stay in school, in one spot, and not get bounced around.

Moyer came to Nucla, liked it and decided he could slowly but surely work his way back into full-time cowboying. It was hard because he wasn't from the area, nobody knew him. He's worked on the Silverhawk Ranch for five different owners. After three years he made cow boss. Dan claims he's still learning and gives credit to cowboys better than he. He learns from them and takes pride in that.

Anything having to do with cows is Dan's decision. In a sense, all the other cowboys work for him. He's the foreman but is called the cow boss. Different places he'd be called a jigger boss. His butt is on the line because when there's a decision to be - it's his decision.

Dan breaks and trains his own horses and occasionally sells them. He works with his family to make a living any way they can. In many ways they're better off than when he was an ironworker - life here is steady and they are fortunate to buy a place and accumulate stuff. Dan reiterates that all he ever wanted to be is a cowboy.

Some of the greatest cowboys Dan worked with tried truck driving, mining or heavy equipment operating at some point in their lives. A real cowboy may have to do other things to make ends meet, according to Dan, but always goes back to cowboying because it's his first love.

Dan loves his job, has a great boss. When he's out on his horse working cattle on a cold morning, Dan appreciates being able to be there. He laments the fact there's fewer ranches in the West each year.

"Look at the American cowboy, these ranchers -- you talk about tradition -- we've got it here right now. If we're not careful we'll let it slip away. Every time you turn around there's a big ranch selling out, turning into a housing development. In my opinion our country is poorer because of it. Now you've got a housing development and you'll never bring back that tradition. It is gone and it will never be back," Moyer states emphatically. "I'm going to stick with it as long as I can.

"What it amounts to is today's land prices are so high that a person can make way more money by selling his land. You can't make as much money with cattle as you can with real estate. I've got a friend in Snowmass with one of the last remaining working ranches who can't make a living because taxes and costs are so high, but if he sells the land it's worth $8 million. It'll sell and it'll be gone, not just the ranch, but an entire way of life, the traditions, the culture," Moyer says sadly.

Land costs, development, federal and environmental attempts to raise grazing fees on public lands all contribute to destroying traditions and a way of life that embodies the heart of western culture.

"It's like the end of the movie 'Monty Walsh,' where the ranch has been sold and everybody scatters, and this guy asks this cowboy what he's going to do and the cowboy says: 'As long as there's one cowboy left to punch one cow -- it ain't over,' and that exactly how I feel," says Dan Moyer, cow boss.

Trees For Future Generations

Forest Service Replants In Sanborn Park

So far this spring our infamous Rocky Mountain weather has turned weekends into bone-chilling, nose-numbing, finger-tingling experiences. This past Sunday held true to form.

Jan Hackett, our resident reforestation expert, gave me directions to planting sites on Sanborn Park and I took off in search of tree planters Sunday afternoon, after the Stanley Cup game was over. It was cold enough to play hockey here.

She was right on with her directions. First left on the flats after the climb up Sanborn Park showed lots of tire tracks. A mile or two down the dirt road and I encountered an obvious tree planters' camp. Scattered over a half-mile or so were visqueen shelters, tents, campers, camp kitchens and cook fires. It reminded me of tree planting 20 years ago, when I did it for a living.

A little way down the dirt, the tracks turn right up the hill into an area devastated by fire with scarred black carcasses of ponderosa standing like sharpened charred perpendicular reminders of the death of a forest.

Dirt turns to rock as the angle of the track increased. I spotted three mud-spattered 4X trucks parked at free will angles with planters huddled against searing wind and traces of snow. These are the slackers, the ones who gave it up and decided to rest rather than plant.

A spotted dog comes over to check me out. I assume he ascertains I'm OK. He lifts his leg and pees on the left rear tire.

"That means you've been accepted," a female voice from inside one of the trucks says.

I scratch the spotted dog on the ears. He doesn't bite me. Good dog.

The voice belongs to a tall, wiry, slight young woman named "Saint." Not Saint Joan or Barbara Saint or The Saint or A Saint. Just Saint. Her smile, which fills her dirty, gaunt face with light, radiates like a 52 Buick grill in benevolent communication with the cosmos.

Saint's hands are encrusted with layers of dirt, like the hands of the rest of the crew. Her hair is some dark, indistinguishable color, matted, wild; her skin is sunburnt, windburnt, weather beaten, parched. Her comrades share similar characteristics.

More planters straggle in, exhausted, ready to give it up for today. More dogs show with each planter. I scratch one of the new arrivals on the ear. He yelps. I quickly withdraw my hand.

"There's a big dog in camp chewed on him," Saint explains, "and don't even try to pet the dog coming in now."

I take her word and don't.

Two-dozen planters from the Southwest Forestry Workers Cooperative work this planting job for the United States Forest Service. The co-op, based in Bernalillo, NM, has been worker-owned since 1977. They do reforestation, forestry consulting, windbreaks, fencing, erosion control, mine reclamation, wetlands, trails and surveying, and native planting.

They bid for USFS contracts on a competitive basis with other planting outfits, own their own tools, equipment and attitudes. Problems are worked out over the campfire or during regularly scheduled crew meetings. Everyone has an equal say.

They proudly wear t-shirts with the motto "STAND OUT AND RESIST." Each is considered an independent contractor. Implied respect is apparent in the way they treat each other. One of the crew serves as liaison with USFS representatives but that's as far as that person's authority goes.

When jobs are successful the co-op reinvests profits into the business. New members are accepted on a temporary basis at half pay until they prove themselves. Like with any family business, it helps to know somebody to get in the coop.

The ground on this job is nasty, rocky and planting isn't easy especially with the dry, windy conditions this spring. Bitter cold makes it worse but planters work every day to finish the contract in the allotted time to the satisfaction of the USFS inspectors.

Jay Nettles, a tattooed, pony-tailed blonde youngster plants in a sleeveless sweatshirt oblivious to the weather. He swings his hoe dad like a combination John Henry and Johnny Appleseed. He's been with the coop for two months.

"It's honest work," is all he says as he keeps the arc of his hoe dad steady, planting the last of his seedlings.

These ponderosa seedlings started as cones in local forests, were collected, germinated and grown in a Nebraska nursery, trucked by semi to Sanborn Park where they're being planted by a crew of independent, wild, tough, hard working young Americans from New Mexico.

I'm particularly careful not to step on freshly planted seedlings on my way back to the truck and the heater. It is snowing harder. There is hope, respect and reason in what's left of the West today.

A Placerville Lifetime

Doris Ruffe Remembers The Old days At The Placerville Corner

Doris Ruffe remembers Placerville when it was the largest cattle shipping point in Colorado, when the center of town was at the crossroads where her father's automobile dealership stood, when what we know today as Placerville was known as Newtown.

Placerville was a hopping town back then with a railroad spur, a Conoco and Texaco station and a three-story hotel, which Doris' great-grandparents owned. That hotel put up 125 miners, ranch hands and workers.

The hotel burned and Doris' grandparents built another. Her father, Glen, ran the garage in town and sold Nash and Studebaker originally, and later Chrysler, Plymouth and GMC. The building at the crossroads over Leopard Creek is what's left of Glen Ruffe's car dealership.

Where the dealership stands was known as Old Town. Newtown is present-day Placerville and Lower Placerville remains the same.

Doris worked for the Post Office for 28 years in Placerville and maintains that the new post office, which was the original livery stable, was necessary since the old one had been housed for decades in what is now Leopard Liquors.

"There's been such a changing group of people over the years," says Doris, "but you have to get to know every one of them because in their own way they're all so very nice, they're just different. They're people who come from the city. Whenever I see anybody I say 'Hi' and the new people would look at me kind of funny and wonder why I was doing that.

"Then the hippies came," Doris recounts, "and some people were so against the hippies but you know dad treated everybody the same way. He'd help anyone, do anything for them. You don't do that to be repaid but it sure pays you back.

"The hippies were different but there was nothing wrong with them. They're good people. Like I said, you just have to get to know people. And that's how things work. People come in and they thank you so much for being nice and helping them and you appreciate it. You help somebody and people turn around and help you the same way."

Doris remembers a winter day when she locked herself out of house and car. She didn't know what to so she called Fender Mender and they came from Norwood and unlocked her car so she could get her keys. She asked Gary what it was going to cost and he told her it was on the house because Kelly'd kill him if Gary charged Doris.

Doris has been helping people in San Miguel County most of her life. She worked with her dad in the garage and helped him with the dealership after she graduated from high school. She worked at the Placerville Post Office and helped out at Mary's Store. Doris has been helping local residents with a variety of paperwork problems at the San Miguel County Clerks Office in Telluride for the last 14 years. Doris never turns you down, never tells you "NO". Doris always finds a solution and sends you on your way with a smile.

She attended grade school through high school in Montrose. Doris lived with her mother in Montrose during the school year and spent her summers with her dad in Placerville. The family was in Placerville weekends and summers and in Montrose the rest of the time so Doris feels she missed a lot of local history in those years.

When she graduated from high school Doris moved to Placerville and helped Glen with the garage doing mechanical work. She remembers helping Glen replace a burned-out motor in a brand-new car. She did whatever it took to help him.

After her father died Doris tried to keep the dealership running but it was too expensive to maintain.

"You had to have all the service tools," she says, "infrared and all these computer things like they have now plus they'd charge you $500 a month advertising, the same as the big city dealerships. There was no way I could do that so I let it go. I did sell some used cars for a while."

There was an eclectic collection of lovely, rusted old cars behind the dealership in the field below the road. There was a Hupmobile, a Lincoln Zephyr, several old Buicks, a Packard. Darryl Elder hauled most of them off and some were sold to collectors.

"A guy by the name of Stan Francis got the Hupmobile and the Lincoln Zephyr. I sold a '41 Packard club coupe to a man in Colorado Springs. He'd had a completely restored 4-door and somebody broadsided him. He came and got my car and rebuilt it from parts from both," says Doris. "He'll come up every so often and he'll stop at the courthouse and I'll come out and look at his car."

Doris still owns a cherry 1961 300G Chrysler and a 1953 Chevrolet that are like money in the bank. She claims she's going to sell them one of these days because she can't give the cars the care they deserve but so far that day hasn't arrived.

"The 300G has a 413 V8 with long rams and two four-barrels," she explains. "Several years ago there was a man from back East and he had two sons aged 10 and 12 and he wanted to look under the hood so he could show his boys because they just don't make cars like that anymore."

"Years ago we had a master technician's course from Chrysler and every month you had a booklet with an update on the new things and Dad and all the mechanics were supposed to take the course. Well I'd do the course and answer all the questions. Much of the time I wouldn't have been able to fix it but when they had problems I'd tell daddy and the mechanics how to fix it," she confesses.

"It's so different with all the new people anymore. Take Mary's Store for example, used to be the only time you'd have a line was when a load of kids off a bus would come in. Now there's a line all the time with all the workers who travel on the road. The only time there was much traffic on the road as there is now was on the evening of the Fourth of July. It is like that all the time now. Now there's people driving all the way from Grand Junction to work in Telluride. Years ago they would have said you were crazy. I can remember the time when

I thought I was crazy to drive to work in Telluride every day. You just didn't do things like that, " Doris explains.

"During the hippies days there were so many people hitching rides. When dad went up to county commissioners meetings in Telluride he'd always have a pickup full by the time he got to town. It's getting to be where there's so many people around here you have to be careful what you do. Of course the shuttle helps because then you don't feel bad about passing them up. I'd pick up anybody I knew and for a while I was known as the Placerville taxi," she says.

Doris feels that the county could save money on the shuttle system by running more vehicles on bad weather days and not running a shuttle mid-day since it's often empty.

"Of course we always drove wherever we went so it's hard for me to put up my car and ride the shuttle," Doris states.

"I get a kick out of all the people living on the mesas. That's how it was years ago. Dad would go up on Hastings Mesa to the dances. There were whole communities up there. It's kind of like a big turn-around after so many years. I'd like to take a trip around the county and meet all these people. That's what I miss about not working the post office Saturdays—I'd get to see all the people."

"This is home. There's ducks down on the river and there were deer in my yard last night," Doris says. "I can't understand people who retire and first thing they sell out and go somewhere else. Pretty soon they're right back."

"You go down through the years and it seems like our friendships and our sense of community aren't there anymore but when it comes down to reality, the nitty gritty, why then people are always there to help," say Doris. "This is a great place to live and people are the same no matter what. Maybe they're a little busier so they don't have as much time for you but no matter how important they are they're still the same people. People here know you, no matter who you are. When it comes down to it they're there for you."

The Youngest Of The Old Timers

Johnny Stevens Looks At Telluride, Past And Present

Johnny Stevens' parents moved to Ouray from Northern California as part of the war effort in 1943. The country needed minerals to fight a common enemy and Americans in those days participated in their wars in both military and public life. Things haven't been that clear in over 50 years.

Johnny Stevens was supposed be born in Ouray but due to a huge mine accident he was born in Montrose. Johnny's earliest memories of both Ouray and Telluride are of the culture, ethnic strength and diversity in the region.

Back in those days Telluride was a community not unlike New York or Chicago in that it was filled with ethnic neighborhoods. There were Swedes, Finns, Poles, Irish, Italians and Germans who brought the richness of their cultures with them.

"Today we're so integrated, so homogenized," says Stevens, "but one of my earliest memories is of all these diverse ethnic groups in the little town of Telluride and the respect they had together as a community. When I was being raised, Telluride was probably four or five hundred people."

John was raised and remains Catholic and in his youth served as an altar boy. This was a serious undertaking in those days and you served until you were 18.

"We married and buried everybody who came through here. I remember all the old people in Telluride and the inordinate amount of widows, which was a result of accidents in the mines. Today the median age in Telluride is probably 42. When I was being raised here there were young people and old people and a few in the middle.

Death became very much part of our lives. I claim I never got much of an education because I was always at church burying people," Stevens claims.

"Telluride was particularly unique," Johnny continues, "because we were at the end of the road. The only people who came to Telluride in those days were lost or relatives. People didn't come to Telluride, Colorado. We had two events a year—Fourth of July and Christmas and everything in between was work, work, work.

"Part of what I miss about Telluride is that there's no old people now. The saddest story to be told in Telluride, and Telluride existed for nearly a hundred years before the ski area in 69-72, is there was a political shift where it was assumed that the old timers knew nothing. The old timers were literally pushed out of this community politically and to this day a lot of them don't understand why.

"They're upset about it. They're the ones who nurtured this place for a hundred years—themselves, their parents. Most of all of the old timers were absolutely one hundred percent supportive of the ski area. We didn't have a bunch of those people who say they don't want anything. We knew we had to have some diversity and we collectively chose the ski industry.

"If you read a prospectus written in the community today it seems like there's a paradigm written about the past and the world begins with the ski area in 1972.

"The old timers didn't want plaques and busts of themselves but they did want to be included. This was their home and now virtually all of them have been forced out. A lot of them live in Montrose but they still love Telluride.

"Then there was a whole different culture 32 miles west of Telluride in Norwood—ranchers, ranchers, ranchers. When the ranching and farming ran onto hard times a lot of the guys I worked with in the mines would work night shifts in the mines and all day on the farm. This was in the 50's and 60's. They supplemented their industry with mining. We had a cross-cultural work ethic. We worked together and played together. It was a unified community. Every high school game meant something. We worked and if and when we got a chance, we played.

"In 1972 that all turned around. It was recreation first and work second. It turned almost immediately. The politics changed, the ethics changed, the values changed.

"Most of the people who came to work in the mines emigrated from Europe because things were so bad they felt compelled to leave. And if you asked these people why they came to Telluride to work in the Tomboy Mine, they'd tell you it was because they had freedom here. If they had to work 14 hours a day to keep that freedom they did it.

"One of my main jobs in high school was delivering groceries. In the 60's there were three markets in Telluride: Goldsworthy's, Pilcher's and Rose's. It was a sustainable community up until the 70's.

"Some of the old folks would call in their grocery order and it was my job to deliver the order to their house. They'd call because they were old, because it was a service, and sometimes just to have somebody come see'em.

"George Cappis brought the first TV into Telluride in the green building out by the ballpark and on Saturday nights the community would show up to watch Lawrence Welk.

"Before '72 you served on the school board as a matter of civic responsibility and pride and not for political reasons.

"There were only a couple or three times the mine was closed in a hundred years. When we won the state basketball championship, they closed the mine so people could come watch us. We were the first team to make it to the state championships. Our parents and the entire community followed us all over the state.

"Telluride was incredibly close. We were miners and didn't have a lot of time for diversions. This community took care of itself. We had a network. It sounds so damned corny but that's the way Telluride was. That era's behind us but what that era left is people not respecting the cultures that were handed down. As a general ethic and a general value a lot of what's worthwhile about the past has gone by the wayside.

"There's just this lack of civility in Telluride today, a lack of respect.

""What's going on is a national and international problem and a lot of communities are trying to reinvent themselves based upon not politics, not money but on community, respect, involvement. It's a great trend that's happening and I see it in Telluride, and Norwood, Ouray, Montrose.

"I don't think Telluride has done that badly relative to other ski resorts, relative to growth in the West but I think what most people are concerned about is the politics that separate us. I think that the newspapers sometimes exacerbate the problem. I know people who, in order to have a good day, refuse to read any newspapers.

"Our single greatest common denominator is that everybody at least cares. Telluride isn't very mature in the sense that if they don't like you, they don't communicate with you and then they get further behind. That's what I think our biggest problem is.

"Our paradigm is if we count on politics and bureaucracies, which we've used as our own scapegoat in this community, we're going to fail miserably. I think people are also finding out we'd better get together. It's a matter of necessity.

"We need to understand that we should never take anything or anyone for granted. We need to recognize the people who've stayed and helped make this town what it is. Our kids need to respect the ski bums who came here 25 years ago and have patrolled the slopes and raised their families here, the people who built and maintained this town through all the hard times and growing pains.

"We need to keep the spirit and the people who literally built the ski business. Building this thing was not easy.

"We have festivals for everybody else. Why don't we have a Respect Festival, a Respectival. We don't need to invite everybody here. Just go introduce yourself to somebody you'd like to know and spend some time with them. Call somebody you know but haven't got together with for a while. We also need more long tables so people would talk with each other. Open the dialogue.

"It's a matter of survival. Once everybody here became successful we became provincial. The town tried to run everything. East End politics is raising the level of West End politics. We all need each other.

"What we decide and implement in the next two years will determine what happens in the next 15 or 20. Growth is coming and we need to plan for it or else it'll flatten us. We need to be incredibly realistic with our economy, accept reality and deal with the future in a finite way."

The Master Builder Reflects

Dirk DePagter Looks At 21 Years in San Miguel County

"Never trust a fat man in a poor country," is Dirk DePagter's rule of thumb for traveling.

DePagter traveled continually for seven years before he and his then wife-to-be Patrice arrived in Telluride in September 1975.

They lived out of their van, looked for housing before winter got really serious and intended to stay for the ski season and move on. They were down to a few hundred bucks and Patrice came up with ten dollars for a license so they could get married and Dirk could remain in the country. They never left.

Places to live were just as tough to find as they are now. The DePagters found a place in a drafty trailer out by the cemetery after the previous occupant had committed suicide on the premises. Dirk never told Patrice the circumstances of their good fortune and they made it through their first winter.

DePagter recognized a situation in Telluride tailor-made for his Old World carpentry and construction skills. His Dutch entrepreneurial sensibilities came to life and Dirk started Dutch Masters Construction.

Twenty-one years later Dirk and Patrice live in the "Dutch Embassy" with daughters Brigitte and Rhea high above Telluride on Last Dollar.

Dirk remains Telluride's original Dutch Master among other things.

"I never came here to create a utopia", says Dirk, "although a lot of people who came to town had a vision that it was possible to create an isolationist republic to rule and regulate without any consequences or without any connection to the rest of the world. This is a very naïve way of looking at life in my opinion. I've traveled all over the world and it was incredibly naïve to think that you could isolate yourself and create an unrelated Shangri-La type of place.

"The fun thing about the town at that time was it was a young community. It was pretty clear at that time what Joe Zoline's objectives were as well as Terry Tice's and Rick Silverman's. You knew what these guys wanted to do and their position hasn't changed. If you want to be stagnant in your attitudes and the way you live, that's fine. It's a matter of personal choice. I'm more pragmatic, obviously, and enjoy experiencing other ideas and attitudes," DePagter explains.

"It became a situation of default," he continues, "as the next winter was a drought winter. Nobody had any money and you couldn't afford to leave town. Draft beers were still 50 cents at the Roma so if you could get two quarters together you went downtown and drank beer. There was almost a rebellion in town when the Roma considered raising their prices to 60 cents.

"The only guy for whom the price of beer never changed was George Kovich. He came in every day, put his 50 cents on the bar and got his beer. One of the things I enjoyed about Telluride at the time were the real old, old timers. There were some classic old timers in town including the last of the breed—Whispering Jim Delpaz.

"That connection was interesting because we live in a community that I call single-generational. There's no interconnection of this generation to generations before. The families who are privileged to have family here are few and far between. This creates a whole different dynamic in the community.

"The difference between our community and communities which have a more dimensional situation is that the older people are like mirrors or sounding boards for the current youth. In many ways this community has no specific depth to it. It is very easy for the latest crop of liberals to keep moving in.

"There's also a couple of critical differences between Telluride and the West End. One is clearly the layers of generations and the other is that West End are people who work with the land, which gives them a totally different mindset. For the most part people in the East End are urbanites detached from the harsh realities of people who have had to make a living in an agricultural society. And it shows in how we react to land use issues and social issues. People in Telluride have a tendency to drift in and out of town but if you've found your niche in an agrarian situation you're not likely to move on.

"Here I love to make fun of some of the people who were on commissions or boards in this town. They thought they were a godsend for HARC or the planning commission or something and suddenly they realized that life went on without them. They had to therefore move to Denver, San Franciso, Durango, Sante Fe or parts unknown to make a living. Although during the time that they were here they were very critical and strong forces in decision making over other peoples' lives.

"That's why it is interesting how people mature in Telluride. People who came here in the 70's and the 80's have retained their sense of humor and have gone beyond the point of trying to create a utopia and have recognized that reality is with us.

"When people come to Telluride and stay two to seven years they sport an adolescent attitude in that they think they know everything that's good for this community and everything that's going to happen. And they try to beat us over the head with it. They just can't understand how we're so stupid as to not see it their way.

"I really am pleased with living in Telluride. I enjoy the lifestyle very much. The discussion always arises about the loss of community and the separation between rich and poor. It was inevitable that some people would wind up richer than others. The community is incredible. It is very strong. It is probably one of the most dynamic, involved communities you could ever hope to encounter. It is dynamic and changes with different people, time frames, social situations. One of the things I've always appreciated about Telluride is it is just as easy for me to talk to Ron Allred as it is for me to talk with Michael Villagos.

"I try to instill that same attitude in my kids, that they don't judge people by what they wear or what they drive or where they live. I want my girls to interact with people according to who they are. It takes effort because sometimes it is more convenient, more secure for people to relate to people who are in the same social or financial niche, that's a very poor life in my opinion.

"What is unique in Telluride's future is that we have the ability to create an incredible ski and wilderness experience with minimal impact on the environment. I believe there is nothing wrong with developing a specific niche—for instance being known as the absolutely best expert resort. That way you're the best at something. Why are we trying for mediocrity? I have no problem with the current expansion proposal but I believe it should go well beyond that. I personally would like to see serious opportunity for alpine skiing in some of the upper basins.

"The San Juans are some of the most unique mountains in the world. We're so far south we have a tremendous amount of sun, on the same latitude as the Spanish Sahara. It is a lot warmer here and a lot friendlier for people to ski.

"If we give people the opportunity for open basin skiing like you see in Europe, at this southerly latitude with beautiful sun and incredible vistas we're going to be so unique, so world-class, so different. It is something I want to see in my lifetime.

"As we head into the next century I believe that people are going to be looking for not bulk experiences but for individual experiences. People want to remember where they were specifically, not experience that blurs together. That's what I think we need to focus on. I really hope that the ski area expands into the high alpine terrain to make this a truly unique ski resort. If we're not unique we'll lose our share of the economic ski market, like it or not. We have to face reality and recognize that skiing is one of the main driving forces in this region.

"If we think we're going to be economically diversified by manufacturing widgets, we're fooling ourselves. We're too far from any infrastructure. Scott Flyrod is a perfect example. It is wonderful for the repertory theatre company. It is also interesting how quickly it went through different functions. Three years ago we were over there with the governor pressing flesh saying how wonderful it was to diversify local economy. I commend Steve Phinney for trying a social experiment of such magnitude, but it is expensive to operate here, expensive to live and finding reliable employees with a work ethic is damn near impossible. There's a reason for Scott Flyrod being successful in Montrose. People there need steady jobs because that's the life they choose. There's nothing wrong with choosing a different lifestyle. Let's not fool ourselves that we could be manufacturing widgets or gadgets or flyrods and be competitive with the rest of the world.

"Since we are a tourist-based economy, let's try to be the best damned tourist-based economy we can be. If you went to Steamboat,

Aspen, Crested Butte, all those places start to sort of blend together. But—once you've seen the tops of these mountains in Telluride—you remember that. It is the power and the juice. That's what we need to strive for.

"A lot of times I feel we're being manipulated by people who aren't able to look either backward or forward. They have no perspective in life. Many of them are people who are self-centered, who don't allow humanity as a whole to grapple and grow and live. If we don't progress in our thinking, in realizing who we are while we're here and what we're doing with what we have—if we stifle that type of dynamic—what we'll end up with is regression into a medieval mindset, total mediocrity.

"We need to allow ourselves to excel and not expect perfection. But it would be nice if we had the next best thing tomorrow."

DYNAMIC DUO

Bill and Jill Masters, Sheriff and Paramedic

They're the dynamic duo of public service in San Miguel County. He packs a badge and an automatic, she packs a pair of scissors and life saving hands. He's the sheriff and she's a paramedic. They're on call 24 hours a day, 365 days a year.

Despite their chosen professions, obsessions or callings, Jill and Bill Masters find time to raise a family, have a life and love each other.

Bill has been a cop in the county going on 21 years. He started in May of 1975. Jill became an EMT in the county in 1980.

"I became an EMT because my neighbor had a stroke and I felt totally helpless," says Jill. "The paramedic happened because I kept going to more calls and needed to know more, be able to do more. It just evolved. EMS is something that gets in your blood. You get hooked on it. We're adrenaline junkies."

Jill remembers seeing Bill on one of her first calls in Placerville where a young boy had shot himself in the head, a suicide.

"It was a very disturbing call. It was one of my first. Bill and I talked about it later, how it was interesting that we wound up at bad scenes together," says Jill.

Jill claims it wasn't emergency scenes that brought the two of them together although they've known each other since 1978. She insists that it was Arlene Boyd's doing when she invited Bill to a birthday party for Billy Boyd.

Jill and Bill have been married nearly five years.

"We have that kind of background where we'd known each

other and seen each other quite a few times at different scenes. That definitely had something to do with the appeal. We're both that kind of person," says Jill.

"We're also both parents," Bill adds, "and there's a lot of things we share in common."

"Jill was involved in emergency services long before she came to work for the Sheriff's Office," Bill explains. "She was an EMT, an EMTI, paramedic, went through all those steps on her own as a volunteer to provide the services needed for our community.

"We're on call 24 hours a day, every day of the year. We have so many pagers at home: the Placerville pager, the Telluride ambulance pager, Search and Rescue pager, Sheriff's Office pager. All these different things go off when emergencies happen. When the children were younger we had to make a decision about who's going to this call because one of us had to stay with the kids," he continues. "If it was a primary medical call Jill would leave. If it was a law enforcement call, I would leave. And sometimes they would cross and we would have to decide how to do this.

"We have called neighbors before and dropped the kids off and now the girls are old enough to take care of the homestead," Jill adds. "They know enough now to call dispatch and ask 'Do you know where my mom is?'

"Sometimes I think that maybe the kids want to have normal parents but they accept the situation totally. They're used to it and they're very supportive. They help out and understand that there's somebody in more need than they are at the moment," says Bill.

"But on occasion it's also trying, like any parents, it's a little difficult because sometimes we're gone. There's times we're needed, when we're out late trying to get some problem resolved," Bill states.

"One day we were planning to go on a picnic but wound up on a search and rescue all day instead. My son kept insisting he wanted to go on a picnic. I told him he's on a search and rescue with me all day. He still keeps a picture of that event. Obviously it was a big deal to him. He just wanted to whine about not going to the picnic," says Bill the parent.

Jill and Bill's situation isn't that much different that most peoples' in combining family and job although theirs is somewhat more extreme in degree. The family and work are their lives and it certainly helps that everyone involved is understanding, accepting and supportive.

"Emergency services, whether paramedic or law enforcement is a calling, it isn't just a job. It's got to be part of your soul if you're going to do it right. Otherwise you're just a bureaucrat like anybody else," say Bill the sheriff.

"We're in a day and age where you can bring the emergency room in the ambulance to the patient. In San Miguel County, Colorado, the hospital is not coming here. It used to be that the ambulance was the old hearse deal where they were they were either dead or you drove them to the hospital with no attendant in back. Ambulance technology has changed so much that we can actually make a difference before we get them to the hospital," says Jill the paramedic.

"I just feel like I've got so much more knowledge as a paramedic to perform what I consider an invaluable service," she explains. "I envision that someday we'll have a county-wide paramedic service whether it's run by the fire department or sheriff's office. It's all a matter of funding and politics.

"We baby boomers are all getting older here," Bill interjects, "and at this age we're prone to heart attacks. It's the number one killer. And emergency services are going to help save us and hopefully allow us another ten years of life."

"I'd like to see emergency services included in a county-wide budget someday soon so we're not constantly having to do fund raising to provide local life-saving services," says Jill.

Paramedic is the highest level Jill can achieve in emergency medical services but she intends to attend law enforcement school in January.

"It's all part of my being more well-rounded as an emergency care provider," says Jill. "If I respond to a scene as an officer then I'll be better able to deal with the situation with authority."

Bill is an EMT but has no plans to become a paramedic. He's got his hands full being sheriff.

"We live in a small community so emergency personnel need to be cross-trained. We train in search and rescue techniques, wildfire techniques, emergency medical techniques. We all need to understand the rhetoric and procedures of each other's specialties to be effective," the sheriff says, "but I still don't think I'll become a paramedic."

Neighborhood of Strangers

The Masters reduce stress levels inherent to their professions by working out and taking a vacation at least once a year. Time off doesn't happen very often since they're involved in some sort of needful community care situation nearly every day.

"There's a lot of satisfaction in what we do. Many people don't do what they love. We get along really well. We go out on emergency together," explains Jill Masters, mother, wife, paramedic, responsible citizen and rock solid woman.

"We were a little bit concerned at first but found that we work really well closely together. We're a good team. I'm pleased that we can do that so well, " says Bill, "that we can work, play, be husband and wife, parents. We really are happy. Life often isn't easy. We get stressed out, we have bad calls, financial problems. Here it is Christmas and everybody needs presents.

"Every time I slipped and fell in my life I landed on diamonds and Jill is a diamond in my life. I feel fortunate because we really love each other," says Bill Masters, husband, father, sheriff, philosopher and a hell of a man.

A Quarter Century Taking Care Of The Town

Raymond Hughes A Local Fixture

The Telluride Maintenance Department may have to work two shifts on a 24-hour basis just to keep up with the present town demands in the near future.

Raymond Hughes, who has been Streets and Utilities Supervisor in Telluride for 24 years, made that prediction based on recent permanent and transient population increases and the demands those increases exact on his department.

"People expect to see more and more snow removed, more and more of this, more and more of that. We've got seven people and we still can't keep up with the jobs at hand and now we've got more jobs. We have to maintain the freeway and the bicycle path. We put up 200-300 signs a year and have to take them down every spring. We're changing signs almost daily in some places," Hughes said.

"We take care of all the water in town, Hillside, Lawson Hill. We now have seven miles of new sewer line we have to maintain from the Aldosoro project. It's progress. We do everything nobody else wants to do. If any department in this town needs help we're the one who move right in and do it or help them do it," he continues.

"We've got a brand new water plant on Mill Creek and the new sewer plant at Society Turn. We're in charge of cleaning the public restrooms on Main Street. It's just something else we have to do. Look at the building going on around here. We have to meet specifications for any and everything anymore," he states.

"We're trying our best but we keep getting more and more new projects and consequently we get some of them done and some of them don't get completed. Sometimes it takes two years to get something done because something else jumps up and gets a higher priority. The town has created more and more responsibilities for us but they don't give us any more help. The town's growing bigger and bigger and everybody wants theirs done today," Ray explains.

As pertains to the 15mph speed limit in town, Hughes estimates that snow removal, which used to take a day and a half, now takes approximately three days.

"You've got more and more traffic coming through town and the traffic that is moving though town is moving a LOT slower, therefore it cuts your time down being able to load, get your trucks out of there and back. Yes, it costs us a lot of time. I can't get my trucks out of the lowest range and you're blowing more and more smoke, sitting there using more time.

"Our number two priority is to get all that snow hauled off as soon as possible. Number one priority is the freeway. And then they want the bicycle path plowed by at least seven in the morning.

"And people want more and more sanding everywhere in town. They want less PM10 but they want more and more gravel. It's like peeing in the wind. They can't understand why you can't do it but they want it done.

"Right now we have to move all the snow out of the alleys. People are going to want more and more services. If they expect us to keep up with all the stuff they want done with the equipment we have, I know we're going to have to run crews at night and crews in the daytime," says Raymond Hughes, Telluride's overwrought maintenance supervisor.

"The Time Was Right To Come Here"

Christina Peterson—Designer, Artist and Craftsman

Christina Peterson is an independent woman, designer, artist and craftsman, who recently moved her Christina Peterson Design and banner fabrication operation to Norwood. She claims one of the main reasons she moved here is the maverick spirit of the people who live on Wright's Mesa, carrying on the tradition of the pioneers who originally settled the area.

Peterson started out making custom mountaineering equipment with a partner in Aspen in 1973. That progressed into a custom applique' ski clothing line. By 1981 Christina and her partner had a hard time finding studio space available. At that time although there was no ready market for her clothing line so she had to diversify. The festival business in Telluride provided her with an opportunity for work and Christina started making large custom free-span tension structures.

She started Christina Peterson Design in 1988 after the partnership broke up. At that point Christina decided to concentrate totally on the art aspects of the fabric business. She's done most of the big, colorful festival banners across Telluride's Main Street, along with festival stage sets and design work.

"I felt I was getting squeezed out of Telluride, except I never bought into it, never owned anything up there. I've been looking at Norwood for a long time and finally realized the time was right to come over here. There are a lot of opportunities that still exist here," says Christina. "So now I'm here."

Peterson moved her studio and workshop to the Galloway Building on Grand Avenue June 1. Her 2,000 square-foot space is a semi-chaotic artful arrangement of industrial sewing machines, large completed fabric art projects hanging from walls and ceiling, glass-topped layout tables and bolts of nylon fabric of very imaginable shade.

Christina employed twelve people while she was running her business in Aspen. With applied marketing and enough work, she feels she has the capability to hire people again.

Besides her fabric business, Christina was involved in the Telluride arts scene. She was on the board of the Telluride Arts and Humanities Council for two years.

"I really have enjoyed coming here and leaving all that behind," says the artist. "The thing that we're realizing is that there is a whole arts community in Norwood. It's a quiet and solid community. This is really exciting. There's a lot of opportunity and support for artists here.

"I make festival banners but I also do the Bluegrass set design which involves things other than banners. I did all the set design for the Wild West Weekend. My work is used for the Jazz Celebration. I've done stages for Bill Graham, another for a San Francisco festival at the Palace of Fine Arts. The International Design Festival in Aspen uses my work annually, as does the Aspen Jazz Festival and the Winter Park All-American Festival. I've also worked for the Blake Street Baseball Club, a sports bar in Denver. I do a lot of different things.

"This is a whole new, growing industry with immense opportunity. Fabric is being used for building and design aspects where traditional applications aren't possible. Denver International Airport is an example. What I have discovered is that there is a lot of technical expertise in the field but not a lot of creative expertise. This provides people like me, who have a creative slant, a wide-open market.

"As far as creativity goes, there are a lot of stock, screen-printed banners out there. What I do is custom applique' 200 denier nylon so it has a real stained glass effect. Everything I do is sewn rather than printed. It's really durable.

"The other aspect of this, which I am just beginning to get into is to use the same banner concept for interior installation pieces. I've done large curtains and free-hanging art pieces. I recent completed a project for Susan St. James.

"My art pieces just come out of me. I don't ever sit down and draw a piece out from scratch because I need room to move while I'm sewing. If I had to work off a drawing, it would be really boring. I think about pieces for days before I get the attitude to actually sit down and execute them. A lot of the work on the piece is mental work before you get down and do the physical work.

"I'm ready to make a stand, to have a home somewhere and I really like this community. If it's possible for me to make it work here, I'm ready to go for it and establish myself here. It would require serious marketing effort. I'm inspired to market what I'm doing and get enough special orders to carry me through the winter into next summer.

"There's a music multi-media conference in Austin, Texas, in March, which I have been thinking of attending for years. I'm really considering going, getting a booth and marketing my work. If that happens, who knows what kind of response I could get. I have the ability, the creativity, the equipment, the inspiration, a reasonable place to work. What I need now is to market my work on a broader scale. I have concentrated mostly on Colorado, Telluride and Aspen. It's time to break out and go for it throughout the Southwest.

"It's an environmentally friendly, exciting business. It's simple. It's the kind of thing you can do in Norwood very easily. All you deal with is UPS and don't need access to a big city. I have suppliers all over the country but most have offices in Denver so I can get supplies on short notice. I have all the seeds but it's just a matter of how I want to make it grow. Marketing is the key.

"Right now I'm working on a commissioned set of banners for the altar at Christ Church, completing a set of commissioned banners for the Telluride High School and doing a banner for the Independent Film Festival in Telluride in January. There is work here.

"It makes a lot of sense to me to work out of Norwood. The wonderful aspect of this is that I have established myself regionally since '81. In this community I don't have to go look for work, people call me. I already have an established customer base here. It's just a matter of broadening that base. I think this can become a really viable business in this community.

""I think a lot of people in Norwood haven't discovered how

really enabled they are. What we as a community need to do is get together and see what we have to offer and what we can do right here to make it possible to have people stay, work and call their own shots.

"The people who came to the San Miguel Basin in the late 1800's were people who wanted to call their own shots. I think their spirit is alive here today. I think that's why we're all here. This is really a community of mavericks and we should honor and celebrate that rather than become something we're not. The possibilities here are exciting."

The Art Of Teaching Art

Jackson Ordean

When Jackson Ordean was in the seventh grade his art teacher gave him a C- for a project if Jackson promised he'd never come back.

Jackson was devastated and the teacher made an impression on him, which he carries with him to this day.

Jackson liked art and artistic things as a kid. He loved to make stuff. He once made what he imagined to be the inside of a submarine out of a cigar box and sent it to the president. Jackson sent a little airplane he'd made to Harry Truman.

There were always successful artists in Jackson's life while he was growing up. His stepfather's father was a successful desert painter. Another friend of the family was a successful western painter and another a successful portrait painter.

Ordean grew up in Laguna, California, which was a bastion of Beatnik art in the 50's. Jackson felt he just didn't have it. He focused on making model airplanes because to him flying was the coolest thing in the world. He was going to an aeronautical engineer.

"Airplanes taking off and Sophia Loren were on the same level when I was a kid," says Ordean. "I would just read airplane magazines all summer long."

All through his childhood Jackson could make out precise visual details but couldn't make out what people were talking about.

"I'd look at people and see their mouth moving, see the pimples, the creases, the hairs in their nose, everything, but I didn't know what the hell they were talking about," Ordean explains. "But I saw everything."

It took Jackson years to figure out that he was a visual person

125

and not a failure at what others considered success. He didn't lack ability or passion or brains. What Jackson faced was lack of confidence. Jackson decided to can the aeronautical engineer idea to something like auto mechanics to get by in life.

It was while he was working on a camper project in the army Jackson decided he could be a shop teacher after he got out. Unfortunately all the shop classes at the time were closed. Jackson was working on an early out.

"There was no way they were going to get a second war out of me," Jackson says, "I learned to finagle and scheme and do everything I could to get out of there."

It was in the army that Jackson came to the realization that he could do whatever he wanted to do.

"I got through the army and figured I could do anything—ANYTHING. There was nothing I couldn't do. They had suppressed me to such a point that I realized that anything I wanted to do I could do," Jackson says with emphasis. "I would have been happy picking up bottles on the side of the road if I could get away from them."

He signed up for art classes in junior college after his discharge. He no longer had problems hearing things. All his assignments were turned in on time. Jackson was working 60 hours a week making surfboard blanks besides going to school. Jackson pulled straight A's in all his art classes. He liked painting but grew weary of the intellectualizing and over-analysis in that department.

"Then I got into ceramics," he says, "because in that department they were happy if you put things together in an artistic way. I was succeeding in that because I worked real hard at it."

While he was getting a degree in art Jackson was also working on getting a teaching certification and making pottery. He made his own kilns, wheels and clay while making a living as a potter in Laguna.

His first teaching job, however, was teaching English.

"That was a good job teaching Chicano kids. I really enjoyed them. They were perfect candidates for somebody to pay attention to them. I did real well teaching remedial English to kids who couldn't pass regular English," Jackson recalls. "I was jumping out of airplanes and then the principal was an ex-Marine and he thought I was great. Seeking the good life, the clean life, the family experience, my wife Moreta and I came here thinking we were going to be part of the big boom and build stuff," the teacher relates, "but it was like running in front of a Mack truck hoping the truck runs out of gas."

By that point Jackson had given up art because it was part of a life he no longer wanted to live. The boom hadn't materialized and people were heading to Texas or the coasts to make a living.

"Up comes this job in the newspaper advertising for an art teacher in Norwood. I came over for an interview. They liked me and hired me as a long-term sub in 1981. I had never taught below the ninth grade and suddenly I've got kindergarteners and first, second and third graders. I had to really shuffle fast. I failed with the small kids at first because I tried to make them do things that were just too hard. It was a struggle. The superintendent finally decided he liked me after three years," Jackson explains.

"I decided that I am a good teacher and did know art better than most of the people in this whole territory at the time," he continues. "It is real human life expression at its most basic and elemental, vigorous level and people deserve to be able to live it that way. Ten years later I'm the art hero in Norwood."

"What I've fought here from the beginning is the antiquated notion that art is a gift you're born with and do well and the rest of us just poke along barely doing anything and are miserable That's pure bull pucky. What I've been teaching since day one is that you don't have to be a genius to do art. If you want to do it I can teach it to you and you'll be happy with yourself and the results. Art is the medium with which I try to teach people that they're worth something, that they're never worthless because God didn't make any junk," says the teacher.

"I put the kids through a certain amount of structure teaching them that they've got to be continually working because they need to get through the course to realize they need to create something of their own," Ordean states. "If I have a hundred students in the class there's bound to be a hundred right answers. My job is to get that right answer for that person out of them. There's times you have to be really patient and other times you have to lift people and help them along so they can get to the point where they'll do it themselves."

"A lot of times art winds up being a dumping ground for kids. They're put in art class because people think it'll be easy on them. Well, it's not. I don't ever make it easy on anybody. It's just different. You've got to take care of yourself, learn to read, get your head into what you're doing and if you don't do that what happens is you get janitorial OJT. I put them to work cleaning. If you resist that and try to do nothing wasting everybody's time, especially yours, I'll give you detention. If you won't do the job for me here, you'll do it after school. I have that power. I don't screw around with people because I want them to get where they can be successful," Jackson says.

"I always indicate to every kid they can go as high as they're willing to work for. Probably my two hottest kids are kids that weren't great when they were little. They had desire. They didn't have the ability to see or manipulate materials but they had heart and intelligence. They're gone far beyond everybody else and they weren't gifted little kids. What really frustrates me is people who know they can excel but won't," he states.

"Even though I don't see myself as a gifted teacher, I still know I'm meant to be a teacher. I can't help but teach wherever I go. I have to. It's not to make myself important. It is sharing," Jackson concludes.

That C- and rejection Jackson Ordean received in the seventh grade made an impression. He has devoted the rest of his life to doing something about it.

Putting Children First

John Mansfield Makes A Difference

Juvenile diversion has traditionally been an alternative to court proceedings. It is a voluntary program designed to allow juveniles in trouble to make a choice. Some kids prefer to go to court.

John Mansfield has run the program in San Miguel and Ouray Counties for seven years. He previously worked as both a teacher and a cop.

"I tell the kids if they feel like they're getting railroaded, if they really didn't do this, not to be afraid of court. 'Go to court and if you can't afford a lawyer, one will be appointed for you.' It is not something to be afraid of. Your side will be heard. The judges will listen to you," Mansfield says.

What John's program offers kids is basically the same thing as the court, with the notable exception that all records are erased, literally shredded when the juvenile fulfills his or her obligations, offers restitution, apology to the victims, community service to make it right with the insistence the kids stay out of trouble and do well in school.

"What has developed over seven years of getting to know the people in the schools and parents is that they'll often call me and ask for help with their kids, if their kids are developing a bad attitude about home or school. They'll want to just talk with the kids. I really like that because that way I'm not a cop," says John.

"The approach I use when talking with the kids is there are a million ways to get where you want to go. One is not necessarily right for all people. Staying in normal public school may not be right for you. There are alternatives like the Job Corps or GED. You can make a positive there. Don't just sit in school, flunk everything and develop an attitude. Face straight on what you want to do and where you want to be when you're 21 or 29. Picture yourself getting a job you want to go to, that you're excited about doing," Mansfield says.

The kids don't often have an answer right away but it gets them to thinking about it. John isn't concerned about how they get there as long as THERE is something the kids are starting to work on. Hanging out, doing nothing is dying, according to Mansfield. Doing anything positive will work for the kids.

"If you're not doing well at school," says John, "don't get defeated by it. We'll talk about it. Maybe we can help with tutors. Maybe the traditional teaching method isn't right. The Job Corps has a different teaching method with a very high success rate with kids who are not typically scholars. And they'll give you a trade, room and board, and a lot of good stuff. You've got to have the guts to try something different and make it work for you. That's positive."

"A lot of my approach with kids is to get them started thinking about what do you really want to do," explains John the counselor. "Don't keep living your life reacting. That's letting somebody else run your life. You have to determine what your road is here."

John feels he was hired seven years ago because he has a teaching and police background. He has more years in teaching than police work but the combination was intriguing to people. He thought that he'd employ the police side of it more but found he uses teaching and mentorship aspects a majority of the time.

"In a sense it is handy to have the police background because I know how hard and cruel the law can get," Mansfield explains, "if you go far enough down that road. We spend a lot of time trying to rehabilitate kids, caring about them. I tell them that somewhere down that road if the legal system decides that you're in fact a criminal and that's what you're choosing to do, they will not care for you anymore. And it is scary. I've watched kids that have backed into it. They get in a lockup for something relatively small and the kid screws up there and it is back into court and a higher security lockup. Often a kid is in that continuing scenario forever due originally to something relatively insignificant."

One way John connects with kids is by taking them on river trips in spring and summer. He lets them operate their own kayaks to teach them that everything they do on the river is significant. He'll advise them how to run a series of rapids but they have to make their decisions and choices themselves. If they do right then they're successful. In they don't then they're in for a dunking and maybe a few bruises.

"It's not a Disneyland ride," says John, "it's their own boat. It's real life. The consequences are real and impartial. We all take care of each other. They pack their own lunch in the kayak. They decide where to stop. They make their own camps. It's a really nice setting. We've had a lot of success using the outdoors with kids. They learn that everything they do matters."

John also takes kids on archeological trips with Fred Blackburn out of Cortez. Blackburn taught at the alternative school in Durango and is a good archeologist who really knows kids, according to Mansfield. John also takes the kids fishing.

"The most important part of all this, what I started to realize and it's pretty obvious, is that the more quality time I'd get to spend with a kid, the better the results I'd get. It's like having a favorite uncle who's always the same guy and he likes you. It dawned on me that's what Partners does," Mansfield declares. San Miguel County was included into the regional program a few years ago and it's been great. It's really taken off. The adult volunteers have been just marvelous. They're great people—people who volunteer their time for kids. It's become a very important part of juvenile diversion for me."

"I think the kids around here are fine," John concludes, "they're like kids anywhere. They do what kids have always done. They're stretching out to become adults and sometimes they make good choices and sometimes they make bad choices. That's why juvenile diversion is in place—if you want to make it right and get on with your life you shouldn't have to live the rest of your life with a record."

Profile: Norwood's Voc-Ag Teacher, Jona Fury...

Commitment To The Future of Ranching And Farming In The West End

She can weld a certifiable bead, craft a folding wooden stool, operate a computer, fix plumbing and deal with futures in the commodities market.

And that's not all. Jona Fury has a Master's degree in Agriculture and is developing the Voc-Ag program at Norwood High School.

Fury considers the study of agriculture one of the most important things a person can do.

"We feed and clothe the world," she states simply.

This is Jona's first semester as Voc-Ag teacher and she finds her students enthusiastic.

Fury grew up on a farm in Dove Creek. She always knew she wanted to be in agriculture. She studied Animal Sciences and Ag Business at Colorado State University, where she graduated with a Bachelor of Science in 1993. After sitting out a semester, Jona started graduate school. She completed her Masters in August, the week before school started.

"A full Ag program encompasses adult education as well as secondary education. I really want to start an adult education program here. There's the Colorado Young Farmers Educational Association and also a national young farmers educational association. Credit for those programs usually runs through community or junior colleges. The Ag teacher does the actual instruction and makes sure there are at least 30 hours offered during the year," Fury says.

"If they want to do something on irrigation or calving difficulty, anything like that, they can ask to have someone come in and talk about whatever it is. They decide what the topics are," she explains.

In the secondary program Jona teaches everything from animal sciences to plant and crop sciences, soil conservation, and mechanics including welding and farm construction. The program is a progressive one where students who come in this year will stay with the program for four years.

"By the time the students are seniors, they're able to do the stuff that's really advanced," the Ag teacher states, "because they've got three years of background already. Each year we build on the information we've done before."

Jona's classes will do things in animal production, soil science, plant and crop sciences, ag business and commodities marketing.

"I'll have the kids pick a certain commodity and track it, track the highs and lows, openings and closings. They buy and sell. They learn how to trade on the futures market," Jona continues. "With the Ag4 class I want to do a marketing program. The will actually form their own business. They develop a product that they think will be useful to the ag community. They have to design and build it, set it up in a local business, do advertising, marketing, take orders for their product and go through the whole process.

"Most of the younger students are very enthusiastic about this program in Norwood. The program is for grades 9 through 12. I want to come meet their parents. The kids all want to get out into the shop. They all want to weld.

"We have all kinds of different little projects. We have a project that will have them learn everything about plumbing. They have to learn how to solder with copper pipe. They do all the measuring and fitting and the final test is when they hook it up whether it leaks or not. Our woodworking project, a small folding stool, will teach them about working with another facet of design and mechanics. The students are excited. They see new opportunities with this program and want to make it work really well.

"I'm starting to schedule home visits. Our teachers schedule three home visits a year and that part kind of freaks the kids out. They want to know why I want to come meet their parents. They want to know what I'm going to tell them.

"What happens is that each student is required to have a supervised agricultural program, an individualized program for every student that allows them to get experience in an area they're really interested in. They decide what they want to do, whether they want to raise animals or crops or work for someone who does. Or they can work in an ag business of some kind. Or they can start their own ag business. I go out and gauge their progress, visit with mom an dad about how the project is coming along.

"It's been really great here. For one thing, I'm closer to my family than I have been in a long time. The community here is really great. The people have welcomed me very well. It was an easy transition for me. I see a really great ag program, one we can be really proud of in four or five years. It should take a while to get it to where it should be.

"I certainly think studying farming and ranching is a viable pursuit for our students. If we can spur enough interest in our kids then they will keep the ranching and farming going. If kids haven't any background in it and don't see what opportunities are, then they go into other fields.

"I feel that agriculture is the most important thing in the world. We feed and clothe the world. Period. It has to continue. Technology will continue to make agriculture more efficient and productive. I don't think agriculture will always be a moneymaker for everyone who is in it. It's extremely cyclic. We're definitely on the bottom of the beef cycle right now. It's a very risky business. People in farming and ranching who are using different marketing strategies are the ones who are making it. Hopefully I can teach that to the kids.

"Agriculturalists are the conservationists. They are the people who are interested in the environment. They're the ones who are interested in conserving the water and the soil. That's how we make our living. Why would you want to lose the very things you make your living with?"

Working The Gold

Artist Mike Baer Follows His Muse

Mike Baer remembers leaving nose prints on pawn and jewelry shop windows. He left those prints because he stuck his face right against the glass in awe of how it was possible to create such beautiful work.

Mike's been at the bench as a goldsmith, artist and craftsman for 22 years. He's an accomplished designer, fabricator, stone setter, caster and freehand engraver. Nineteen of Mike's 22 years at the bench have been spent in San Miguel County. His studio is located in back of Bear Paw Books on Grand Avenue in Norwood. Mike's wife Frances runs the bookstore while Mike smiths in back.

"After the Vietnam War I knew I didn't want to work in a factory. Arts and crafts attracted me and I tried lampshades, embroidery, toothpick sculptures, pottery, all of which didn't last," says Baer.

"Then I went nosing around jewelry studios and just couldn't get enough. I studied that in art school at the University of Wisconsin one semester shy of a degree. I couldn't stand it anymore, took an apprenticeship and started doing it full time," Mike explains.

"It went well. I was following the art fair circuit when I came to Colorado for the first time. I went to see Steve Benham, an old pal who was my foreman when I was a goldsmith apprentice. I still had no idea I'd stay. I did some other regional art shows and came back to Colorado and discovered that the guy I came to visit had starved that whole winter," the goldsmith continues.

"That was '76 and '77 and they were all leaving. The closest goldsmith was in Montrose. It was wide open. I decided to stay. Looked like there was lots of easy money.

"Who could have predicted that gold would go over $800 an ounce in 1980? My phone quit ringing. I went to my pal Dirk DePagter and asked what I could do on a construction site with no experience and no tools. He told me to buy a staple gun and had me hanging fiberglass insulation because nobody else wanted to do it.

"With poverty coming in the back door I watched my wife and my life and everything else walk out the front door. I sat there for a month with the lights out eating fried beans, calling around to people I had worked with. I followed this trade to Los Angeles. I became lead smith for E.H. Bohlin's in Hollywood.

"Bohlin's makes everything for the movie industry that's made of leather or gold or silver with gems. They make the most expensive, fanciest and most correct saddles in the whole world. I mean, $75,000 for a saddle? Everybody who came in through the front door was easily recognizable.

"One of the reasons I came back here was because living in LA at night is no way to go. It just isn't fit to live there. Even if I couldn't make a living in Colorado, I knew I could eat because Colorado's crawling with food.

"For a while I pursued the mountain man lifestyle and it was interesting. I learned how to shoot one of those monster black powder guns. I made a costume that was practical. My hat was made out of the raccoon that had killed four of my chickens. I traded an elk hide for some earrings and made leggings out of that. My good old pal Smokey Moore made some correct, period-type, Apache-style moccasin boots. I still have all that stuff. I just don't hunt big game anymore. It got real political, rather than getting together to share ideas about mountain men. It wasn't what I had in mind.

"Now hunters bring me animal parts, which I can mount in silver and gold. Everything that's got teeth, claws, horn, antler, can be made into something special to the person who's having it made. Everything you've ever seen that's made with turquoise would look just as nice with a tip of elk ivory. Elk have two ivory teeth. Bailey Collins brought in four teeth from one elk. I made a watch band for him. Just when you think you've got Mother Nature figured out, she fools you.

"From Florida to Oregon, hunters have given me orders for what they want, half the money and when it's finished I ship it to them.

I've got 100% happy campers. I've already got four orders from hunters this year. One of them just brought his family jewelry in to get fixed because he couldn't find any jewelers that he liked.

"The major portion of my work is doing people's custom orders. They'll come in with an idea and something that's special to them and we'll figure out how to translate that into silver or gold so they can wear it.

"This is the only the only thing I've ever done with my hands that's never been boring. Not even for a minute. It's a constant challenge and I improve daily, even after all this time. You have to stay in practice or you lose it. Take hand engraving, for instance. I have to do it at least a couple times a week if I want to stay good at it. Hand engraving is just not done anymore.

"My best ideas come as I wake, right as I come into consciousness. I keep pencil and paper close by because sometimes the ideas are so fleeting that they might be gone if I don't make some kind of notation.

""I've got to have a 100% satisfied customer, to the point where they're not only satisfied but bragging about me. I've got to have that happen every time.

"Before I get old and go blind I'd love to pass this on to a variety of people. If some of these skills aren't passed on they'll be gone. It's still viable to do it this way. I have taken on apprentices in the past. I hope to take on more. I always hope that the person I train doesn't compete with me within a block of where I'm working. It's not that much to ask."

When I asked Mike Baer if he had any awesome words of wisdom to impart he had this to say: "I think there's a real big similarity to this trade and unicorns and mermaids."

He's got one tattooed on either forearm.

Kamchatka

Knute Hylan carries a tomahawk with him on his forays away from camp onto the Kamchatkan tundra. One evening before he heads out, one of his fellow expedition members asks why he takes the tomahawk.

"So I can kill myself in case I get attacked by a bear," Knute replies.

Knute and Don Proebstel are in Kamchatka on a fishing expedition in the Siberian outback, looking to substantiate reports of cutthroat trout on the Russian landmass.

As far as anyone knows, there are no cutthroat trout in Siberia. There are reports. Proebstel is the president of the World Salmonid Research Institute and Hylan operations director. They were invited to Kamchatka by members of the Russian Academy of Sciences to research and classify salmonid fishes. Proebstel has been to Kamchatka and other parts of Siberia several times before. He's doing his PhD. dissertation on the Siberian lenok, a type of Siberian trout, as a doctoral candidate in ichthyology at Colorado State University.

The Kamchatkan Peninsula, roughly the size of California, Oregon and Washington combined, lies directly across the Bering Sea from Alaska at the tip of the Aleutian Archipelago, separated from Siberia proper by the Okhotsk Sea, north and west of China and Japan. It is the land of volcanoes, geothermal activity, tundra, the world's largest bears, the world's largest eagles, and some of the world's largest and most unusual trout.

Kamchatka is populated with 400,000 people and 300,000 live in the coastal city of Petropavlovsk. The ethnic mix is made up of indigenous peoples, Russians and Orientals. Knute is amazed there is no hot water in a city of 300,000. Apparently the Kamchatkans have a central hot water system, which works sporadically, although Thai hookers work Korean bars continuously, according to Knute.

The expedition to the town of Esso on the remote eastern slope of Kamchatka along the Sredinny Hrebet, the backbone of the volcanic mountain range, which splits the peninsula, requires flights in surplus Russian military helicopters. After that it's a raft trip down the Tigil River through uncharted rapids. Later the expedition mounts into a surplus Russian armored personnel carrier column for a wild ride over the tundra, crossing rivers, fishing their way to the coast.

The expedition, comprised of members of the Russian Academy of Sciences, Knute and Don, along with members of the Wild Salmon Center based in Seattle, pick up two bear hunters, Volodya and Misha when they get to the eastern slope. Volodya is Russian and Misha is Ukrainian. They're along on the expedition to ensure that Kamchatkan bears, which are among the largest in the world, don't have expedition members for lunch. Recently a famous American photographer, famous for his bear photographs, was attacked, killed and eaten by a Kamchatkan bear. Apparently he disregarded sensible behavior while camping and what little was left of him was shipped home in a bag.

Knute fishes for the first time in his life on the expedition. He catches steelhead, lenok, rainbow, grayling and char of extraordinary size. While Knute fishes, Don and his Russian counterpart do taxonomic work for later DNA study. As luck would have it, one of the Russians catches the cutthroat they've come all this way to find and the fish is now at the Russian Academy of Sciences in Moscow. This is an important find in the world of taxonomy and salmonid research.

The expedition spends over three weeks in the outback. Camping on the tundra is no easy task since bears rule and a man without serious firepower is like a flashing sign in the wilderness to "Eat At Joe's." Kamchatkan bears stand over 10 feet tall when they survey their domain. Knute says it's an impressive sight.

On the tundra, the expedition camps in abandoned cabins built by escapees from the Siberian gulags decades ago. The escaped prisoners of Soviet regimes preferred to face the Kamchatkan wilderness rather than life in the gulags. The cabins afford at least minimal protection from marauding bears. Armed expedition members take turns guarding the camp at night, while a huge fire burns to warn bears away.

Neighborhood of Strangers

Knute begins forays away from camp alone, his sense of bravado enhanced by his ability to survive the expedition intact to this point. He is further bolstered by the double barreled 12 gauge shotgun he carries along with a few extra rounds, given to him by the Russians so he doesn't have to kill himself with his tomahawk if he encounters a bear.

One evening towards the end of the expedition he's out alone with his shotgun and six rounds when he sees a bear standing a hundred yards away, smelling, searching. The bear drops and lopes towards Knute. No use to run. The bear can outrun him. He checks the shotgun and grips extra rounds between the fingers of his left hand. He tries to control the adrenaline rush come over him.

Staccato bursts of 7.62 sniper rounds hit the bear in the chest. The bear falls to the tundra, dead. Misha, the Ukrainian bear hunter, checks the bear before he checks on Knute.

Saving The Fish

World Class Research

Two former long-time residents of San Miguel County have dedicated themselves to the conservation and research of salmonid fishes around the world.

Don Proebstel and Knute Hylan have been instrumental in the creation and development of the World Salmonid Research Institute, a non-profit organization based in Rollinsville, Colorado.

Proebstel is president of the institute. Hylan is director of operations.

The idea for the institute originated with Dr. Robert S. Behnke, a professor of Fishery and Wildlife Biology at Colorado State University, and president of the institute.

Behnke is a world authority on the classification of salmonid fishes, author of NATIVE TROUT OF NORTH AMERICA, and editor of the English translation of two Russian scientific journals, The Journal of Lethyology and the Journal of Hydrobiology.

Dr. Behnke's encyclopedic knowledge of western North American trout is legendary. An avid fisherman himself, he is a regular contributor to many fishing magazines. Throughout his career he has championed the diversity of Western trout and promoted the wise management of this irreplaceable resource.

According to Dr. Behnke, the idea for the institute originated over 40 years ago while he was working with Russian scientists on classification, conservation and management of salmonid fishes. Over two thirds of salmonid fishes in the world live on the Russian landmass with a majority living in Siberia.

Proebstel is a doctoral candidate in ichthyology at CSU and Dr. Behnke's protégé. After doing research in Siberia with icthyological counterparts from the Russian Institute of Science in Moscow, Proebstel orchestrated the inception of Dr. Behnke's brainchild.

With Hylan's help, Proebstel sought out investors, arranged for the purchase of Manchester Lake outside Rollinsville and incorporated as a non-profit organization dedicated to the conservation and research of salmonid fishes on a world-class, worldwide scale and the World Salmonid Institute was born.

The institute is involved in a regional program to bring back the Colorado Greenbacked Cutthroat trout, a wild, native Colorado species, which recently was taken off the Endangered Species list. Research facilities presently include a hatchery and the institute's dive team is conducting a systematic study of Manchester Lake as habitat for Greenback Cutthroat and Rainbow trout. Knute Hylan is in charge of the institute's dive team.

"The family salmonidae is a large family of primitive fishes which originated about 100 million years ago. The family includes both Atlantic and Pacific salmon, all the trout, honcho and lenok. The honcho or taimen includes the largest salmonid that's ever been caught in 1952 in a river in Siberia. The fish weighed 105 kilograms, which is somewhere around 240 pounds. This is a freshwater trout. Two years ago the biggest salmonid caught by an angler in Siberia came in at 92 pounds. The big ones are still out there. It's an important resource to conserve and that's why we started this institute," says Proebstel.

Don is doing his PhD. thesis on the Siberian lenok.

"They're the trout of Siberia. Their range is enormous, from the Pacific Ocean to the Arctic Ocean, all the way into Mongolia and China, probably ten times that of the Western trout in North America that we're all familiar with," he explains.

According to Proebstel, there are more rare genera, one of which exists in a lake in Siberia created by a meteor three million years ago. The fish lives at depths exceeding 300 meters.

"Our goal with the institute is to take it from a scientific angle," says Proebstel. "We have a board of scientific advisors, which include the top people in the world. Along with Dr. Behnke, we have members of the Academy of Sciences in Moscow, the top salmonid biologists in

Russia and the head of ichthyology at Moscow State University. These are all members of the institute. We have scientific advisors from Idaho, Utah, BYU, and the National Fisheries Service in Seattle.

"We tried to assemble a list of scientific advisors who are members of the institute in principle, who support our goals and who hopefully will become active in research programs we can initiate.

"We want to pull in support from fishermen, private parties, and industry that are dependent on these trout and salmon for their living. We have a vested interest I keeping the family salmonidae around.

"Our ultimate purpose is to conserve the resource. The way we're different is that we want to take a scientific perspective and do really legitimate scientific research with a goal of conservation in the long run.

"There's no secret what happened in North America. We've lost almost 98% of native cutthroat trout. Even rainbow trout in their native range are in trouble in a lot of places. We're losing runs of salmon and steelhead in the Columbia Basin, which used to be one of the great bastions of salmon and steelhead in the world. Now only 2% to 5% of the fish left in the Columbia Basin are actually wild, doing what they evolved to do. What we're trying to do is take a global perspective on this issue.

"There were people who had good intentions when they brought Brook trout to Colorado around 1880. They didn't consider that the brook trout might impact the native Cutthroat, which were so beautiful here. What we'd like to do is take the benefit of our experiences to more remote places in the world that haven't been impacted yet and try to protect those resources so we don't continue to make the same mistakes.

"It's important to realize that salmon are a keystone organism, meaning the whole ecosystem depends on them to function properly. Two million sockeye salmon run up a river in the Kamchatka peninsula annually, for example. They're born in that river, run out to the ocean, gain energy and biomass, and bring it back to the fresh water for all eagles, bears and other organisms to live on. There's more than just a selfish perspective that we want to be able to fish for them. There's a really important purely biological reason to conserve the family salmonidae. We're trying to conserve an entire natural cyclical dynamic.

"We've had the experiences of seeing what happens when we change the natural dynamic. We need economic development and harvesting of replenishable, natural resources. We also need balance.

"The reason why we actually formalized the institute is that there really isn't one group which takes scientific perspective and is supported and funded by private citizens, anglers and industry to benefit from the best available knowledge and techniques to make reasonable decisions to lobby for well-funded conservation ideas and methods to become reality.

"From a scientific point of view we can easily come up with reasons, objectives and means of conservation but we also need some dollars and power behind us to actually enact programs which will make a difference.

"The organization is new, we've only been incorporated for a couple of years. It's taken that time to get a scientific board in place. We definitely have the best salmonid biologists in the world on our board. There's still a lot of work to do. Now we need some key power players from manufacturing and industry."

KINDNESS

The biggest fish caught during a recent fishing and research expedition to the Eastern Slope was in the basement of the Colorado State University Veterinary Building in Ft. Collins on a scorching Friday afternoon.

I wangled an interview with Dr. Robert Behnke, America's foremost salmonid taxonomist. Behnke knows more about trout and related fish than anybody in the States, probably the world. I was on my way to the interview with an old buddy from the early days of Telluride. He was a lead singer in a rock'n'roll band, involved in a continuum of the best looking women any man could hope for. The one he's with now can stop your heart and kick-start it with a twitch.

Don Proebstel is no longer a rock and roll singer. He went to school and is working on a PhD. in ichthyology at Colorado State University. He's my connection to Behnke, a dissertation away from his PhD. working on DNA identification of fishes for the Colorado Department of Wildlife.

Proebstel has put together a nonprofit organization dedicated to worldwide research of salmonid fishes. The organization is called The World Salmonid Research Institute.

The institute is located outside Rollinsville, Colorado, and they're dedicated to saving the Greenbacked Colorado Cutthroat trout, which is presently on the endangered species list. The greenback is one of the few remaining native Colorado trout.

Don put together investors, bought land along with 25-acre Manchester Lake and got together with scientists from the Soviet Academy of Science in Moscow to do research on salmonid fishes.

Don explains the workings of the institute with expertise

on salmonid fishes. He tells stories about fishing in Siberia and the Kamchatka Peninsula, explains the origins of whirling disease, lays out fundamentals of DNA identification processes and provides background on Bob Behnke. Behnke has chosen Don for his protégé, no mean accomplishment.

All through this barrage of information I see the Don of old on the stage singing "and all the federales say they could have had him any day, they only let him slip away out of kindness, I suppose."

Finally we get to Behnke's office in the basement of the veterinary building, not a square inch of space not filled with periodicals, books, specimens, studies and floor to ceiling with every imaginable source or reference on salmonid fishes, 5-gallon jars of specimen trout yellowing in decades-old alcohol, their entwined, fish-eyed features grisly in magnification. Some of the books are in Russian. I'm reading through the titles as Behnke walks into his lair.

He's in his mid-60's, sporting a smile only a lifetime of nonpretension can assure. When he speaks he's like an uncle imparting solid stuff. I ask him about whirling disease. He launches into a major explanation in terms I can understand although I'm sure he could have upped the rhetoric and left me in the dust.

Partially through the interview I indicate I'd like to take some photographs. He picks up on it and an unusual angle. My meanderings bring me to a corner where I spot a mounted fish big enough to make me stammer, a 17lb., 37" cutthroat caught by W.S. Green, Sr. with his son, W.S. Jr., at North Lake, Colorado, in July 1917. W.S. Sr., gave the mounted fish to Behnke.

As I look to Behnke, he nods, anticipating my question. I pull the behemoth out and place it in front of Behnke and Proebstel for a photograph, a perfect situation combining past, present, future with the aid of the unpretentious master.

Behnke tells us we can take the fish for the institute. He lets it slip away out of kindness, I suppose.

DRUGFISH

A redneck pal swears local fly fishermen practice catch and release because Telluride dumps effluent into the San Miguel River and the fish are on drugs. He's appalled I keep and eat fish out of the San Miguel.

Dr. Robert Behnke, America's foremost salmonid taxonomist who has worked in fisheries biology for over 40 years, internationally recognized as one of the leading authorities on salmonid fishes explains the problem is more complex than fish on drugs.

According to the taxonomist whirling disease is being much discussed since it began affecting the economy of trout fishing around the world, although the disease has been around as long as trout.

The mistozoan parasite that causes the disease lives in the tubifex worm and feeds on fish cartilage. The tubifex worm thrives in the silt of river bottoms. The parasite does not affect humans.

The parasite gets in the fish and starts to migrate towards the head and cartilage. The damage is done during an amoeba-like stage of the parasite when it feeds on the cartilage before the bone is formed. The destroyed cartilage, especially around the nerve fibers, causes the whirling gyrations in fish.

In the wild, when fish have a fright response, they react like a dervish. There's almost no survival in the wild. According to Behnke, once the fish get enough infection to get to the whirling stage they're effectively dead.

If a rainbow trout hatches out in a tributary with boulders and gravel in it there's probably going to be very few, if any, tubifex in it. Then there's a good chance they'll survive without whirling disease infection. By the time they come down to the main river, or get to an area where the tubifex is, they may be large enough to resist the disease. They may get infected but it won't affect them.

Brown trout are not completely resistant. If brown trout get a high enough infection they can display all the symptoms too. There's a very high incidence of brown trout in the Colorado River with the disease. Most brown trout are just much more resistant than rainbows. There was one brown trout found with 600,000 whirling disease spores in it and seemed perfectly healthy.

Whirling disease affects almost all salmonid fishes but the impact varies greatly. Brook trout, rainbow trout, and cutthroat trout are probably most susceptible. The only trout the disease hasn't affected are lake trout. Lake trout are evidently so genetically different they haven't been affected. Of course, they don't live in rivers.

Something that's completely unknown at this time is that some strains of trout may have developed resistance, which may include whirling disease. Everyone hopes that maybe there are wild rainbow trout someplace that have developed that type of resistance.

The wild rainbow trout in the Truckee River in California have flourished despite evidence of whirling disease for 30 years. There are reports of whirling disease from as far away as South Africa. Everywhere trout have been stocked there's whirling disease.

It's hopeless as far as getting rid of it. Once there are trout and tubifex there's going to be whirling disease. Hopefully we can come up with a strain that's resistant.

The resistance could be evolved fairly rapidly in those strains that have been surviving. Right now the damage whirling disease has done is not going to be a simple resistance as insects to insecticide. A lot of that kind of resistance comes from one gene. For years hatcheries have bred resistance to different diseases. Whirling disease is very complex so chances of success aren't imminent. It'll take strains of wild fish with hereditary resistance, like the Truckee River rainbow trout that have been living with the disease for decades.

The most controversial question is stocking of diseased fish in waters where it's already occurring. Putting more diseased fish in the river is a proverbial drop in the bucket. As long as there's trout in that river you're not going to get rid of that disease. The potential rate for multiplication of that mistozoan parasite is enormous. A dead fish releases hundreds of thousands of spores. Potential increase is not going to matter, it's not going to lower the infection rate. Stocking is not going to lower or increase disease levels as long as the disease is contained only where it occurs now.

This is the best argument for catch and release I've heard. Add drug-addled effluent in the water trout live in and catch and release is a shoo-in. Golf, anyone?

Solar Power—An Alternative

Electrical Storm On Hastings Mesa
Part 1

There's been an electrical storm brewing over Hastings Mesa for years. Three totally solar developments, Old Elam Ranch, San Juan Vista, and Hastings Estates have opted not to allow grid power.

Mesa residents are opposed to San Miguel Power Association establishing power lines on the mesa. They have fought grid power for philosophical, environmental, emotional, historical, esthetic and lifestyle reasons.

There has never been grid power on the mesa. The people who live there now want to keep it that way. Oleh Lysiak begins a series of interviews with Hastings Mesa residents this week with Rita Robinson, who has lived there for nearly 20 years.

Robinson is a professional counselor, former news director of KOTO, who, with late husband Brian Rapp, envisioned and started the thousand-acre, all-solar Old Elam Ranch. She is presently building a home on the ranch.

"We got a good deal on the property. Then we had to design the water system that would serve the development, which was the greatest challenge because there wasn't any way we could do one well for 35 acres. We spent a lot of time and energy developing a water system and pumping it with solar panels. This was unheard of at the time. This project has been used as a national example of one application of solar. It works," says Robinson.

"We did not, as developers, determine that this should become a solar community. It was really the people who built and bought up here who wanted that to happen. It was their majority vote that

150

determined the issue.

"It's not about people who live solar are good and people who want grid are bad. For me, it's just having a choice. This may be one of the few places in the country where you can have this choice. That's what I think makes Hastings unique. There are not that many places in the country that are off the grid. We live in a huge place with thousands of acres with no power lines. It's a unique situation. There's a real difference between buried power lines and no power lines.

"My issue is that when you do not have an easy source of electricity, you have a very different approach to building and living on the land. You will not see trophy homes on Hastings Mesa because you cannot do them. You have to be more sensitive to the limitations of what solar provides. You cannot have a really big house with no conscious awareness of electrical consumption. You have to at least have some level of awareness.

"Also the reality is that the grid wouldn't change it too dramatically. This is about a lifestyle choice. And it is a choice. I have no problem with people who choose a different lifestyle. I want the option to choose mine. There's something about having this mesa grid-free that is part of my choice.

"Let's face it, we are all part of this problem. The solar panels are a source of pollution when they're built, lead-acid batteries are a problem, generators pollute. I don't think we're some great group who think have found the key, an answer to our environmental problems. We feel this is a step in the right direction with a lifestyle that's more fun. We have fun up here doing all of this. It's a pioneering thing also. It's about being independent, self-sufficient. I never have to worry about a power outage. I like that feeling.

"You don't always need a generator. Some people don't have their systems designed quite right. We're still learning up here. There's something wrong with systems where people have to use their generator more than 5% of the time. Wind generators are nice because they are a great backup for solar.

"Hastings Mesa has attracted a unique group of people. People who made a conscious choice to live off the grid. We all have our own reasons but we have this alternative approach in common. Forcing the grid on a group of people who don't want it is in a way saying 'you can't have this lifestyle.'

"The people who bought up here in the first place knew they were buying into a place that didn't have electricity. They were taking a chance. There are people who only want electricity because they think it'll increase their land value. People have a right to do that because this is still America. They do not have a right to do that at the expense of people who are making this mesa their home.

"As a developer of this ranch I have not suffered because we do not have electricity up here. The fact is that it is not an economic disadvantage to not have grid power. Here on the ranch we use the fact that we're a solar community as a marketing tool. We attract only the people who find that intriguing. The property on Old Elam and all over Hastings has appreciated dramatically. With or without electricity this land is valuable.

"It sounds like we're being really exclusive up here but what we want is a choice. There are plenty of other places people can build whatever they want and have all the electricity they want to suck up.

"There is an economic issue here. It doesn't make economic sense for San Miguel Power to build a power line into a location where the majority of the people do not want it and will not hook into it because they already have their electricity and can't afford to hook up into the power line anyway. Why should consumers be paying for that trunk line? Is that fair? If any of it is San Miguel Power's expense I have a problem making the consumers pay.

"We are part of the problem so I don't want to get self-righteous about the whole thing. We can only do the best we can. Take the water issue for instance. What I was most afraid of is that we were going to pump the aquifer dry. We have some pretty strict water regulations on this land, which are unheard of on mesas. Electricity is one thing but up here the real gold is water.

"When we bought this land we actually did, against my personal wishes, look at the cost of bringing power up to the land. It's a responsible thing to do as a developer. You have to look at the economics of everything. The economics didn't pan out.

"We can go on an on about what we believe philosophically but economics are a determining factor. In the end economics have to take into account environmental considerations because it will cost more and more to get power from fossil fuel. In the long run we are looking at a less expensive power source.

That's how things will change in this country and on this mesa. Fossil fuels are a limited resource. I love to plug in my appliances. I love plugging in what I need and go right on using the sun.

"We're going forward, not backward. We're creating a new life-style, not re-creating an old one. I'm not interested in attacking the people who want power up here. I would like to see the actual numbers of what it would cost them to bring grid power up here.

"I value what Hastings Mesa has to offer and a big part of that is that it's not on the grid. It's special. I would like to see that uniqueness acknowledged."

Solar Power—An Alternative

Something Special For The Children
Part 2

Amy and Glen Pihl want to do something special for their children. They want them to be able to see the Milky Way on any given night, whenever they step outside the door of their Hastings Mesa home.

The Pihls built a solar-powered home on Hastings Mesa a couple of years ago and they're thrilled that the San Miguel Power Association has decided not to run a power line over Hastings Mesa. Hopefully the Pihl kids, as well as others on Hastings Mesa, will be able to enjoy the Milky Way for years to come.

"My husband and I designed this house together," says Amy Pihl. "When we bought the land up here we knew we were going to be using alternative energy. It was kind of exciting to think that we could have a nice home here powered by alternative energy. The possibilities are really quite endless as to what you can have on these systems.

"One of the most exciting things for us was that we could be part of research and development for the future, part of a solar community dedicated to a more reasonable lifestyle. The philosophical and practical aspects are very important to us. They're especially important after you become a parent. You want what's best for your children. It's possible to make a better way for the kids," Amy continues. "We have 320 days of sun a year. There's no reason not to utilize it."

"We're a buffer zone to a wilderness area. We're interested in responsible growth," says Glen, a local builder.

"If the grid were to come across here every realtor in the area and their friends would be up here pushing this land like they push land in every other square inch of the county. Actually, the wild nature of the land will eventually become more desirable because of the solar community. Solar power is becoming more economically and technologically feasible every day.

"Our photovoltaic system was $7,000 and we've been here for two years and it works for us. We've got all the amenities including a washer and dryer and even with two kids it works well," Amy interjects.

"I'm afraid if grid power ever comes up here a whole different mentality will come along with it. There's no polite way to say it. We'll have lights on all night. We'll lose the Milky Way. It's really quite nice to be surrounded by people who are conscientious about it. I think when you have a core group of people who are concerned about the same thing, that's not going to change," Amy says.

"In the mid 80's I was involved in research on some lakes in the Adirondacks to determine acidity. The lakes were extremely acidic. I understand from listening to National Public Radio that the acidity in Northeastern and Canadian waters is being attributed to coal-fired power plants in the Midwest. Unless we make a change and go to alternative power-producing sources, we are all responsible for degradation of the environment.

"We want a for all these young ones and to be able to enjoy what we've enjoyed. I think we've got a good chance at making the right things happen. We've got a lot of backing. People want to do what's right," she concludes.

Kris and John Holstrom are the Pihl's neighbors in the Hastings Mesa solar community. John works at the airport and Kris writes an organic gardening column and is an organic gardener extraordinaire. They live in a totally solar home with their two kids, Kirk and Kelsey, and Susana Correia and Nat Stephens, who help with the organic garden.

"We're not anti-growth up here but sure would like to keep the people who do come up here aware of what we're doing. We're the only place around that does this. All the other mesas are electrified," says Kris.

"The main thing that holds us together up here is that we are such a diverse group of people. We all think about where our power comes from so we have a tendency to turn our lights off when we don't really need to use them. To an extent it's a more low-key approach to energy consumption. We have neighbors who have 25 guests on the weekend. It's just a matter of style. It all works," Kris states.

"Also, it's a philosophical thing," John adds. "It's about making a difference and being able to demonstrate that it actually does work. We try to do stuff such as wind generators, which work. When there's no sun there's usually wind. This is an experiment in progress. There's both a philosophical and a practical reason for living in a community such as ours on this mesa.

"The big problem with any possibility of grid power up here is that it would change the nature of the character of the mesa as we know it mainly because of mega or trophy homes. There are some large homes up here now but we certainly don't need any 12,000 square-foot homes in this neighborhood," John states.

"Another thing that we're trying to do as a group is send all area landowners a letter telling them when they're ready to build we'll provide them with information on photovoltaic systems. If they want to know anything from cost to technology then all they need to do is call us and we'll give them all the help, information, ideas and education we possibly can," Kris explains.

"There's a guy on Hastings Mesa, a big-time shrink from Philly who wanted grid power but got converted to solar instead. He looked at the cost of bringing power up from Sawpit and saw that it was more economical to do solar instead. This works," Kris concludes.

Solar Power—An Alternative

Photovoltaics Practical & Reliable
Part 3

The third installment of The Post's solar series, which began with the historical aspects of the solar community on Hastings Mesa and continued with political and philosophical aspects, takes a look at technical and economic applications with a look to the future in an interview with Dana Orzel, a solar designer who works for Johnson Electric Ltd., Montrose, Colorado.

The interview began on an extremely serious note when Orzel spoke about a photovoltaic, wind-backed installation, which powers the radio relay system on Red Mountain.

"The guys who died on Red Mountain died because the radio repeater went down. The highway patrol, road crews and rescue people couldn't talk to them, couldn't find them. They didn't know where to look or what they should look for. The trucks had stopped to assist some motorists and got hit with an avalanche. The relay is located on top of Red Mountain. It went down," says Orzel.

"Now they've got the ability to stay in communication. We were requested to assist in designing what they need up there. We asked them what they required for s system and they said it's a totally life or death situation. They don't ever want it to go down. It's an emotional situation. The people who still drive up there remember the friends they lost," states the solar designer.

"We have in excess of 270 sunny days a year. Solar is a great advantage in Southwestern Colorado. We helped design a photovoltaic, wind-assisted system, which will allow them to stay in communication no matter what," Orzel explains.

Orzel went on to explain that photovoltaic systems are only as good as the quality of components used and the abilities of the people who design and install them. He urges anyone who is thinking of installing a photovoltaic system to employ a designer who actually lives with a photovoltaic system.

"You get what you pay for," he says. "The electrical inspectors for this region are known nationally as the toughest inspectors in the country. The systems which pass inspection around here are the leading edge, the state of the art of systems anywhere in the United States."

Randy Johnson, Orzel's employer, earlier this year attended a task force meeting in Everett, Washington, for the 1999 National Electric Code concerning the Solar Electric section of the National Electric Code. Johnson is the only contractor in the country who was invited to attend the meetings, which are made up of engineers, manufacturers and underwriter laboratories staff, as well as other experts in the solar industry.

"The people who advise us are typically industry people," Orzel continues. "From a technological point of view, photovoltaic is growing up. The industry is involved in standardization with UL. Things have gotten to the point that PV products check and double-check themselves if we're talking about the new inverters. They're able to synchronize themselves to the frequency patters of the generator, if you're using a generator for a backup system.

"Systems today are able to look at so many different situations with the ability to protect themselves from low voltage, high voltage, over-amperage. They have the ability to transfer from inverting power to generating power quick enough that it doesn't shut the computer off. Transfer times have gotten so fast it's amazing.

"Technology has moved forward to the point where industry standardization has made a huge difference. One person manufactures batteries, another inverters, another charge control and the power center. Integration has gotten smoother. The National Electrical Code now spells out the standards, making solar power more accessible. Definition, clarification and specification is allowing photovoltaic to work for everyone today.

"Economically, if you got rid of subsidies for nuclear, hydro and fossil fuel power generation and those industries were forced to compete with photovoltaic or wind-generated power, breakthrough power sources of the future would be viable today.

"There are trophy homes operating totally with solar right now. It all depends on what you're willing to spend. Is it really worth it? That's a kind of decision the customer has to make. We can design and install any kind of system, however large, as long as somebody is willing to pay.

"Southern California Edison and Texas Instruments came out with a roofing shingle that is photovoltaic. You wire them up and what happens is you get a synchronized grid interconnected inverter. Basically, the photovoltaics you pick up off the roof are turned into the AC power you need in your home and the excess is sold off the grid, with no batteries involved. You get rid of storing it yourself. The grid interconnection is already there. What you're doing is trading in and becoming a partner.

"There's no reason why the majority of homes in the southern third, if not the southern half of the United States shouldn't have solar hot water, solar electric. It all boils down to economic viability.

"Wind generation has been limited technologically. Now we have the technology to switch DC to AC so quickly that wind generation is technologically viable. The average wind speed on the mountaintops around here is 26 mph. Every moment of every day, the wind is blowing at least 26 mph. We put a wind generator on Red Mountain as a backup because if we get socked in for a week or two we had to consider what's moving the storm. When the wind hits the mountain, it gets compressed. The system on Red Mountain is designed for 120 mph wind, with gusts of up to 220 mph. Wind is a good backup.

"There's a new wind generator out that lists for about $550. It's equal to about one solar module. One solar module may put out 85 watts in one hour. The wind generator, with a 35 mph wind, can peak at over 500 watts. For the same price you can get four to five times as much power.

"The long view involves grid interconnect. If somebody spends $10,000 to $30,000 as an independent power producer, they invest more per capita than the people who are partners in a utility. The bottom line is that the dollar controls it. If people can get a return on their investment, why not do it?

Neighborhood of Strangers

"As long as people want to live in remote locations, photovoltaics will prosper. It's economically viable in our region. People's power needs differ. There is no average. The cost depends on how much you want and what you can afford. The dollar is still the bottom line. One of the toughest parts of an alternative power system is going through the design process. Most of us aren't conscious of how much power we consume each time we turn on a light switch.

"We look at the item, the quantity, how many hours per day, how many days per week. We come up with a weekly average. It amazes people how much they use.

"People ask what an average solar system will cost. I don't know because I've never met the average person. There are a lot of options out there. Different applications create different results."

15 Years Of Friendship

Five bikers rode 2,300 miles from North Carolina to be at Keith LaQuey's fifteenth annual gathering in Norwood. They're riding 2,300 miles to get back home.

Bruce Cook, one of the cycle enthusiasts from North Carolina, has been a regular at the party for 14 years. This year he brought his 9-year-old son Cody to the cycle clan gathering on the back of his big, shiny black Harley-Davidson.

"When Cody heard I was coming to Keith's party in Colorado, there was no way he'd let me go without him," say Cook.

Bruce met Keith at a bike rally in Daytona, Florida. LaQuey invited Bruce to Norwood. Bruce has been cooking North Carolina style barbeque at LaQuey's party for the past few years.

"The reason we all come," Cook testifies, "because Keith is a hell of a nice guy, not at all phony. He's a real sincere, honest man."

The three riders who accompanied Bruce and Cody, Frank Locke, Pete Efird and Elbert Efird all agree with Bruce. Frank Locke is 67.

"People here have treated us like we're family," both Pete and Elbert attest.

Frank Locke has been coming here for years and brought his wife April so she could experience the extraordinary feeling and atmosphere of this part of Colorado.

The annual LaQuey motorcycle brotherhood gathering began 15 years ago when Keith was building his '48 panhead with Dave McDonald of McDonald Harley-Davidson of Grand Junction. The boys at the shop were going to make a run and wanted to know if they could stop by. That was 15 years ago. The rest is history.

It got so big at one point Keith had to move the rally to the county fairgrounds.

Neighborhood of Strangers

"The neighbors were all cooperative," says county commissioner candidate LaQuey, "but they were curious for the first few years. It was funny. There was a steady chain of cars around the block with rubberneckers checking us out."

"When we moved it to the fairgrounds, we did the whole shot with motorcycle rodeo events. It wasn't the same as having it in the yard. It just got too big. We had it at the fairgrounds only one year. At that point we made it invitation only," Keith explains.

"In the early days it was pretty much an open party. We had guys coming from Wisconsin, Michigan, Oregon, Texas, from all over. This year we've got guys from Belgium. We've got a good cross-section of the scooter community," Keith continues.

"In the last few years the tents have gotten bigger, more comfortable. Some people come in motor homes now. It seems we've gone from wild to wide," Karen LaQuey interjects.

"We've never had any problems. The important thing about these people is the respect that everybody gives one another. We did have an incident a few years back. A girl wandered off from the yard and the cops found her on the steps of the old drugstore. She told them she was waiting for the bus to Salt Lake City. They brought her back to the yard," Keith recalls.

When there were dances at the local bars the guys would push their cycles back to the yard rather than take a chance on getting involved with the local constabulary.

"It just a matter of respect, that's what these people are about. They're basically working-class people. We have people from all walks of life, all ages. We have guys who own their own companies, construction supervisors, lawyers, welders, prize-winning car builders and designers. Most of these guys have known each other for 15—20 years. It's not only respect. It's also love and brotherhood.

"We have a yard boss and a fire chief. After this many years the party runs itself. A couple of the old timers aren't going to be here for health reasons or whatever. We'll miss them.

"What tied these people together is the love of motors and the lifestyle, the freedom that it represents and the respect. Most of the guys build and work on their own bikes It takes a certain tenacity, a certain toughness. It's just a breed.

"The main thing is we all love one another. We don't have an exclusive on that. I've been riding motorcycles of one kind or another for decades. An old pal of mine says that Harley-Davidsons keep a lot of people from going insane. That's especially true if you build an old bike and it lives with you in your house. You look for old parts or get custom parts fabricated. You establish relationships with people all over the country.

"There's characters, everybody's got a story, an individual persona. It's a lot of fun. There are names, nicknames and handles. These are a funny bunch of guys. We've gone through the hardcore period but now have guys in their 40's, 50's and 60's. You ride what you bring. It's not just all Harley-Davidsons. One year we had a guy show up on a Honda 90. We've had Suzuki's, Moto Guzzi's, BMW's and probably every kind of bike made. But we also have some very distinctive, beautiful Harley-Davidsons. Another year we had at least five show bikes that had been in Easy Rider magazine.

"We don't see each other but once a year but I know that if I ever need anything all I have to do is push a button and these guys are there in force. This is definitely family. There's an amazing level of honesty and integrity in this family. And it's also a lot of fun to ride with these men and women. There's a long tradition of scooter women from the motor maids of the 20's, 30's and 40's.

"It takes courage to set out on two wheels with your little bag of tools and a few bucks for gas, not knowing where you'll wind up. It takes a certain kind of person.

"In '65 I broke my leg real bad in a motorcycle wreck. While Karen was visiting me in the hospital she went into labor with Kirsten. They whisked her upstairs and Kirsten was born. Then they wheeled me upstairs and we all went home together. I didn't get another bike until the late 60's.

"The relationship you develop with a machine is really indescribable, especially if you build that machine yourself. I started building my '48 panhead here in Norwood. It lived with us in the dining room. I don't know what it is about the things but it's obviously something in the genetic chain.

"There's love, romance and poetry involved plus it's way cool. The sound, profile, craftsmanship, art all have something to do with it. Some of the creations special builders are coming up with now are really outstanding art, a means of esthetic expression: audio, visual, sculptural, kinetic.

"This is the social event of the season. A lot of local guys show up. There's guys in their 20's now who used to remember this as kids. They used to hang around the fence. The local people have always supported us here. In fact one of the reasons we started Karen's restaurant in '84 is that we didn't have a place to eat. Nobody really felt like scrambling eggs the morning after the party. We needed a place to feed all these people.

"There's nobody more American than a guy on a Harley-Davidson. It's a lot more than a motorcycle. It's the Great American Highway, a kind of freedom you can't find anywhere else, a true blue way of life. We're emulated all over the world.

"The Harley-Davison has transcended the outlaw image. Senator Campbell does it. It's the great American symbol. And it's such an individual statement. It's a curious thing. Long skinny guys ride'em stretched out. Fatboys are built for fat boys, rat bikes are ridden by guys who are rats, guys with long noses. What it comes down to is lack of b.s."

World Class Recycling In Nucla

Burbridge Sets the Standard For Glass

DeeAnna Burbridge earned her PhD. in recycling from the University of Hard Knocks.

"You've got to crawl before you can walk or run in this business," she says.

DeeAnna runs the books, office and personnel for Brubridge Trash Service, Inc., in Naturita, while her husband Bob runs the trucks and the trash and recycling site east of Nucla. She claims she's the "ma" in the "ma and pa" business.

The Burbridge family employs 17 people to collect and recycle trash from Telluride to Disappointment Valley. Three employees work in the office while the rest work in the field or in the mechanics shop on the trucks. The Burbridges started the business in 1973.

They cover all of San Miguel County and from the west end of Montrose County to Slickrock. Their service radius is over 80 miles.

The recycling drop-off center is located east of Nucla, where they buy aluminum. The center is open on Tuesdays from noon to 7 p.m. Glass, newspaper, office paper, cardboard, steel and plastics are recycled there instead of being hauled to the dump.

"It's cost effective because people aren't paying the landfill fee and we end up recycling it," DeeAnna explains.

"Aluminum and steel go to Recla Metals in Montrose, a metal broker. Glass is recycled at the Burbridge shop since they created an end use there.

"We've closed the recycling loop when it comes to glass," DeeAnna explains. "It's generated here, processed here and used here.

We collect glass of all kinds and create a sand product that's 3/8" minus all the way down to a sand blasting grit. It's used for things ranging from soil amendment, aggregate additive, concrete, landscaping, drainage systems and water filtration plants.

"It adds a higher thermal factor to concrete. We had a company from Pasadena, CA, order the glass from us for an additive for adhesives they were using to resurface waterways. We're had people from the Air Force and other waste management entities come look at our pulverizing operation.

"We can use any kind of glass with our pulverizer. Most recycling of glass is restricted to food and beverage jars so they can be turned back into food and beverage jars. They won't take window glass, plate glass, pyrex, ceramics or automobile glass. We can recycle more types of glass. We didn't have to separate colors. I have it in my driveway. It's wonderful because it's so clean, doesn't get muddy, doesn't bog down," the recycling expert continues.

"Most people have this myth about recycling that poof—you put something out and then somebody takes it away and poof—it's back to whatever it was before they took it away. Things don't work like that at all. Recycling is a very complicated process no matter what you're trying to recycle.

"Usually virgin products cost less than taking a product that's already been used, cleaning it up and turning it back into something. Volume dictates where and how you can handle end markets. If you don't have a lot of something, then going to an end market might not be cost effective. Most of the end markets are where the higher population centers are. We're not really close to any higher population centers.

"Metals are easiest because they're less contaminable. Glass we don't have to worry about. Paper we ship to Salt Lake, Denver, Oregon City, OR. In April we decided to support the local broker in Grand Junction and build a network that will support more volumes of recycling in the future.

"We collected 27 tons of cardboard for recycling from February 15 to May 15. It's a lot of cardboard given our rural nature but then we also have a resort nature. Cardboard goes to a cardboard mill in Pruitt, NM.

"From the curbside level we provide customers with 18-gallon bins, whatever their volume of generation. Then they do a source separation. There are two six-yard bins located behind our truck cabs, in front of the compactor. The recyclables go in those bins.

"We collect recyclables at the same time we collect trash. It's more efficient given our rural nature and the low density of the population we have. It's not cost effective for us to collect recyclables separate from the trash.

"Then we bring the recyclables down to our yard where they're emptied into appropriate containers or places for processing. Everything else is separated until we have enough for a bale. Aluminum bales weigh 800-1,000lbs, paper 1,300-1,500lbs, corrugated cardboard 1,000-1,200lbs. We can ship about three bales in a semi load. When we have enough for a load we have to pay to have it shipped to where it needs to go. We're pretty much breaking even with everything we have to ship.

"There's a few things which are necessary to having a successful recycling program. The first is economics. It has got to cost more to throw something away than to recycle it. Federal landfill regulations became more intense in 1993. Colorado was in the top 10 of becoming an approved state to administer their own landfill regulations. That made our county realize that they'd have to start paying to dump their trash. Up until 1991 nobody had to pay anything to throw something away. Recycling wasn't cost effective.

"Demographics are a factor. There's a better level of participation with a higher knowledge of how to recycle. In a resort area people are coming and going constantly and not aware of how we do it here. Location to market is the third element.

"The last element is that of personal choice and education. A lot of times people think that someone else should take care of their problems, they're not personally responsible as a consumer. Every time they go to the grocery store they're making a decision about what they're going to throw away and what they're going to recycle.

"If I have a choice of buying something in aluminum, plastic or glass, I'm going to buy glass because I like the way I can recycle the glass. It's healthier because aluminum deteriorates into the food and plastic is a hard thing to recycle.

"It's one of those situations where people shouldn't look to someone else to fix their problems when it comes to recycling. It's a choice.

"The proposed transfer station at the bottom of Keystone Hill would be a recycling and staging area. I don't know what the volume of plastics coming out of the Telluride area will be. If we don't have that staging area, then it will be harder for us to recycle plastics and subsequently other materials because of the logistics and space involved.

"If we have that staging area somewhere closer than 60 miles away to sort things out and send them in different directions rather than collecting everything in our compactor trucks and driving to the landfill, we can use that time for other environmental projects.

"The majority of our trucks, function and service are in Telluride, Mountain Village and everything above Keystone."

Exporting Trash

It's the same old environmentalist Telluride deal—they're for the environment as far as they can see. After that it's somebody else's business. If they can't see it then it's not a problem for them.

Telluride produces more trash, garbage and hot air than any other part of the county. But they don't want to take care of their own. They want somebody to haul it away so they don't have to deal with it. They'll accept it in anybody else's neighborhood but their own.

Telluride loves its festivals. The festivals are awesome trash-producing events. They sell the public on the fresh air, environment, views and all the rest of the gobbledygook but like spoiled children can't take care of their own mess.

We have a county commissioner who fits that description and another who follows her. These nature lovers are all for the scenic beauty but for the price one needs to pay to maintain it.

We have a planning commission that does the same thing. Their grasp of specifics is limited at best. They'd rather have Burbridge Trash Service anywhere other than here, meaning the bottom of Lawson Hill, where trash could be separated, dealt with, recycling bins and distribution points set up.

Brubridge has spent a lot of time, effort and money on a solution everyone could live with. With a transfer station in proximity to town there would be fewer trash trucks on the road, less traffic, less pollution; health, safety and welfare of the community enhanced.

Instead of telling Burbridge what to do specifically to accomplish goals and Telluride community needs, the planning commission side stepped the issue and gave a subjective song and dance saying the transfer station could be placed at a better location.

Neighborhood of Strangers

What better location? The Burbridges have exhausted suitable locations trying to please the commissioners. Are the commissioners going to step forward and offer a new location in the vicinity? What do you think? Then San Miguel County Board of Commissioners was certainly no help when DeeAnna Brubridge showed with an appeal regarding abuse of discretion by the planning commission.

The only commissioner who made sense at the meeting was Leslie Sherlock, who at least spoke English. She saw there was an abuse of discretion and said so.

Commissioners Anna Zivian and her sidekick Jim Craft danced the shuck and jive horsepucky rag around the real issue, blew some smoke and patted each other on the back.

And the trash still travels 60 miles because Telluride's environmental assessments end at the bottom of the hill.

San Miguel County Commissioner

Leslie Sherlock Listens
—And Speaks Her Mind

Leslie Sherlock listens.

She listens to the pet peeves and problems of 4,000 constituents and does her best to be fair at a time when San Miguel County is going through enormous, unsettling changes.

Growth in the county stands at 10% to 11% when Governor Romer declares that 2% growth is a handful.

"Raymond Snyder said something to me about eight years ago when I was the public and he was a commissioner," says Sherlock. "I used to call and rant and rave about issues I thought were important. He said to me 'You know you don't need to be hostile or angry to get my attention.' I never thought about it, it never occurred to me that I thought I had to be on the verge of hysteria before I called my commissioners. When I was running for office I told him I had taken his advice. It is amazing, you can talk to your elected officials without being enraged and it's actually much more effective.

"People call the county commissioners with an enormous range of things, some of which are probably not appropriate for government to be addressing. I prefer that people work their problems out among themselves because when government is asked to intercede, it ticks everybody off around them," the commissioner says.

"I find most people have one ox to gore and if you help hem gore their ox then that's the only ox they want gored. The problem is there's 4,000 people in this county and that's a lot of oxen to gore," she states.

"San Miguel County is experiencing tremendous growth. When you're dealing with as much growth as we've got, people sometimes want for government to stop the growth and in fact we can't because it's illegal. It's a free market system. You can put planning and zoning in place, which limits growth and density. Most of the people in the Telluride region want zoning because they're starting to feel choked. There is zoning in that region and they actually want more zoning to make sure they're not over-densified.

"They don't want to get so many people in the region that they can't handle the traffic, air quality, water impact, environmental issues. Those are what zoning should be about, not whether you want to allow this many people to live around you. We can legally zone on what the environment can handle.

"If the roads are two lanes and the state is not going to widen them for the next 20 years, you can only put so many cars onto those roads.

"Now the West End is resistant to zoning and until they're ready to be zoned it probably won't be appropriate to zone them. Hopefully it won't be too late at that point to create the zoning, if indeed they ever decide they want it.

"I know this sounds cliché but I want to preserve and protect agriculture. The land use code currently excludes agriculture on everything. Agriculture is not regulated in this county. The way we're trying to preserve it is by keeping it unregulated. The land use code is now set up to stay out of their hair.

"San Miguel County is changing. There's growth due to the popularity of the ski area and growth due to the popularity of Colorado. Therefore I think there's a collision of cultures—the old culture that's been here forever, that I love, and the new people who are coming in. There are efforts among citizens right now to stop government from making decisions or regulations regarding master planning, economic diversification, jails, road impact fees, logging, transportation and parking. Those are all hot tickets right now.

"If government makes no decisions or regulations regarding those issues, no action is a decision too. If there's no action I am concerned that people who have taken no action will let growth take place willy-nilly. Are private property rights more important than good planning? If the majority of the people decide that private property rights are more important than planning for their region on water, traffic, air quality and density, then that's what government should listen to.

"If you don't address these issues it doesn't stop growth or change on Wright's Mesa. Wright's Mesa goals and objectives in their master plan, which was written in the late 70's by old time ranchers, are good. They're simple and straight to the point. They do affect zoning.

"I need to listen carefully to special interest groups while remaining cognizant that I represent over 4,000 people. So when special interest groups come to a meeting because that's their ox to gore, I have to take into consideration everything they're saying but I represent 4,000 people that may not be at that meeting. I have to put everything in perspective.

"I have to take into account all those people who may not have the nerve to go to a public meeting and face angry mobs.

"I'm not a typical politician. I don't have a goal in mind to be a politician. Being an elected official is something I get drawn into because I think I have certain capabilities but it was never a career goal. I like owning and running my own businesses.

"I'm dancing as fast as I can to keep up with all the issues. People say they want less government. With rising costs, I hope people understand that may mean less services. With less government come less services. We've lowered the mill levy in my term by two points. We have downsized government by 5 ½ people but we have the sheriff's department needing new people so we probably are down only one employee because of that increase.

"When people say they want less government they mean they want fewer people pushing paper and more people out building roads. So do I. I work with road and bridge every month. With rising costs, if we can keep our employees where they're at and not get new ones, we'll be doing well because that means you're getting less government. We have to deal with the cost of living in San Miguel County and all the costs of doing business. Less government will mean fewer services so be prepared.

"With the enormous changes happening in the area I think people expect government to stop change rather than monitor and affect change. What government's supposed to do is make sure that funds get appropriated and distributed properly, make sure the money gets into their district, oversee basic government services including road and bridge, parks and recreation, building, planning and social services. They also address legislative issues from the state level.

"If people want less government they need to remember what basic government services are supposed to be and stay focused on those so that we can do those jobs well.

"Lately because of citizens groups need to be very visible and vocal, I have taken enormous beatings at meetings. They say rude, negative, inflammatory things to get the attention of the press and the crowd.

"The elected officials that work on the Norwood town board don't get paid a dime. They don't get paid to be beat up like that. I will continue to listen to the citizens. Absolutely, I will listen to them.

"The worst thing a county commissioner can do is to try to get something done. If you do nothing then you'll probably get re-elected, if that's your goal. If a commissioner tried to go out and do things, then some percentage of the population isn't going to like it and they'll come out and go after them."

Sounds like it's time to listen up and do right on all sides.

An Interview With Gene Rummel

The Norwood town planner has applied to San Miguel County for quitclaim deeds for rights-of-way on several county roads around Norwood. A public meeting on this application will be held by the San Miguel County Planning Commission August 14 in Telluride.

A majority of Wright's Mesa residents who could be affected by "flagpole annexation" have spoken out against this proposed process at previous BOCC work sessions, have taken up petitions against the process and have voiced displeasure with the town's attempts at forced annexation.

Gene Rummel, retired former state road maintenance supervisor, who lives along the Vet Road, doesn't agree with the town's methods or approach to annexation and explained his position in an interview with The Post.

"I think the reason that they're trying to do it is to get more land inside the town boundary and then everybody who is involved in it will be able to make more money on it," said Rummel.

"There's certain people who want to enlarge Norwood without our permission. If you want in someplace and it's feasible, they'll let you in. I think they're going about it the wrong way by trying to push it on us. They should ask people instead of trying to force them.

"I just don't feel like I want to be annexed into the town right now. If they do this now, all the land will be within the city limits in three years and there's nothing we can do about it. They'll be able to do this without a vote on it. That isn't right.

"The state highway department may not know that most of the people involved are against this. The county may not know either.

175

They depend on what Richard Grice and the rest are telling them.

"What's the reasoning for it? It's quite a ways out of town. They just want more and more.

"They'd get a lot more out of people if they just confronted them and be up front about things. I just flat don't believe in flagpole annexation. It's not going to bother the state or the county. If the town annexes these roads it's going to cost them a lot more money to maintain them. Do you have any idea what it costs to maintain a mile of road?

"Maybe everybody should call the highway department and tell them we don't want this and want some hearings on it. Let's tell the highway department they've been misinformed.

"They're holding the P&Z hearing on this in Telluride. That's just another way they have of getting around what the people really want. After the boards and commissions listen to what the people say and go completely against what the people want, somebody has to take responsibility for making those decisions. The people making decisions are supposed to be representing the majority, not a select few. I believe a majority of the people indicated they don't want flagpole annexation. Why is the town of Norwood shoving this down our throats?

"I told Norwood Mayor June Estep and everybody else that I don't think this is right. If the majority of the people don't want it, then the town should leave it alone. It's really none of their concern. It's not their property to be dealing with."

A Visit With Darryl Elder, Fence Artist, Junkyard Master

The automotive history of the San Miguel Basin lies literally in the junkyard fence that Darryl Elder built.

If it's true that good fences make good neighbors, then Darryl Elder is the best neighbor anyone can have because his fence is built of wrecked, abandoned or junked cars and trucks that Darryl's been hauling to his yard since 1957.

The now famous Norwood junkyard fence is artfully stacked three and four high, with automotive specimens of every possible type and description. It runs along a quarter mile of dirt road just slightly north and west of Norwood, a near-epic piece of Americana.

"My dad predicted that I'd pave this acreage in junkers," says Darryl, cap typically askew, squinting out from under the bill, "and I damn near got'er done. I mashed out (sold, cut up, flattened, or shredded car carcasses) three times already but I ain't mashing this time 'till my neighbors sell out or die."

The fence was born in an effort at neighborliness on Darryl's part.

Darryl was born in Norwood, April 30, 1941. He quit high school in his freshman year, went to Nucla for a while, came back to Norwood, tromped construction and ran the yard weekends hauling, stacking and dealing in used parts and chasing women.

His grandfather was a blacksmith who homesteaded the land the Elder junkyard sits on today. Darryl's father was a miner who worked uranium, ran a coal mine on the family property and traded livestock.

"My dad quit mining coal when the market went to hell and everybody converted to natural gas and propane," says Darryl.

Darryl, who works as a truck driver and mechanic for the ski area today, began running the junkyard full time in 1974.

"I hope my boys will take it over someday because there's more money in this than there is working for somebody else," claims Darryl.

Darryl and his wife Mary have three boys and a girl: Darryl Jr., 26, Jim, 17, John, 15, and Betty Mae, 7. The younger Elder children attend school in Norwood. Jim and John help their father in the junkyard.

Elder estimates there are more than 1,500 vehicles in the fence and yard. If you're looking for a particular part, Darryl always knows what pile it's in or else he'll point you in the right direction.

"I'm certain that there's pieces of a Model T here, he chuckles, "and I've got a 1921 Star that runs and a cherry 1952 Chrysler convertible and a 1948 Dodge Power Wagon with 30,000 miles on it."

"If it wasn't for them Chevy's, the yard would be a lot emptier," Darryl claims with disdain, "if you want a good truck, get you a Ford—they'll keep on running."

Darryl is outspoken about newcomers to the area.

"They'll buy 'em 40 acres," he says, "and start to tell us who's been here for generations what to do and how to do it. I'd just as soon they went back to where they come from."

When it comes to the water situation in Norwood, Darryl, who's been a water commissioner says: "We should improve the water we have and not work on water we don't. The town put the screws to the rural people who come up with the water in the first place.

"It was a great county to live in until these &*@!#*@&! come in with their regulations, laws, petitions and all the rest. Now you can't tell what the hell's going on."

Mayors Of The West End— June Estep

"Free for all or not free at all," is the primary philosophy of Norwood's controversial mayor.

June Estep is a capable, smart, tough woman faced with the unenviable tasks of revitalizing Norwood's dilapidated water system while she coaxes the town into the 21st century with a firm hand and a singular vision.

The responsibility didn't fall into her lap. June asked for it when she got herself elected mayor of Norwood.

Most any day finds June holding court in her kitchen in back of Grand Liquors, which she owns and operates with her husband Willard. Phone in hand, she conducts the business of the town around the kitchen table. There's usually a few people with multiple concerns at the table trying to bend the mayor's ear as she fields calls from state officials, grant agencies, friends, co-conspirators, board members or irate citizens.

She's got a quick wit and a ready smile punctuated by world-class dimples. She takes no guff from anybody and is Norwood's own version of a modern-day Mae West.

If you've seen June operate at any number of Norwood's board meetings, you'll recognize that the mayor does her homework, has her version of the facts firmly in hand and presides with authority.

Politics not only makes for strange bedfellows but by its very nature invites criticism. June get her share from various factions who aren't pleased with what her honor is trying to accomplish. Some want to reinstate the past and others wish to undermine the future. Everybody has an equal opportunity to gripe.

"I wish the ones who complain, the ones who show up at decision making time had been there all along while we were working it out," Estep says, "there's any number of boards but I never see the ones who holler most take up the responsibility where it's needed.

"The people who are happy with what's being done don't show up at meetings to tell us how happy they are. They're the silent majority."

June's had her hands full since taking office. She's managed to get Norwood's streets chip sealed, helped arrange the virtually operational state of the new fairgrounds facilities, got a new land use code adopted, arranged for a loan for a major water storage facility, engineered the concept and political reality of Norwood's desperately needed new water system, managed to arrange a light industrial zone, applied for a grant to move and modernize town hall and is working on attracting industry to Norwood so that locals can have jobs.

"We're not going to have smokestack industry here. We're looking for small industry, cottage industry, service industry. What we're proposing isn't such a radical change. We recognize that agriculture is of primary importance in the area. Agriculture is a desirable industry here and is very unrestricted in San Miguel County," says Estep.

The mayor is all for San Miguel Power Association moving its headquarters to Norwood.

"It makes sense," she says, "and so does building the county jail here. I'm just crazy about Norwood."

The mayor claims she's not continually embroiled in controversy.

"Norwood was just recognized as 'Tree City USA,'" she says, "and we have a tree committee and came up with a project people wanted to see."

Estep foresees the eventual demise of the 'good old boy system' in the region where, if you're important, you can get it done and if you're not you can't.

"We can't have that," says the mayor. "We have to have fair laws that apply equally to everybody equally, that's constitutional. If it's OK for me to do it, then it's OK for you to do it and it's OK for the next guy to do it. I'm a real primary use by right kind of person. Let's make it where we can give a yes or no answer."

With a year left to go on her tenure, June can't give an answer whether or not she'll run again. What she really wants is to build her and Willard's place out in the country and live the good life. If that includes being mayor is uncertain at this point.

Estep's comment on her main achievement as mayor: "Hopefully it will be getting things in place where the future's up to the people who live here and not because they're restricted from doing it."

Now you may not agree with her honor's vision or politics. She'll undoubtedly be the first to point out you don't have to.

Guest Commentaries

West End critics need to persuade, not intimidate

Scott Flyrod left town and took its jobs to Montrose. The Uncompahgre Combined Clinics are in the process of federal review. The county commissioners and sheriff are looking elsewhere to build the jail. The San Miguel Power Association is considering possibilities other than Norwood (for a new headquarters building). The town faces a referendum concerning comprehensive zoning and doublewides, which threatens to undo years of work by elected officials and appointed boards.

Our school administrators keep resigning. We can't seem to keep a principal or superintendent. Our dilapidated water system is in critical danger of becoming totally non-functional. There's a water war brewing between Wright's Mesa and the town that's about to erupt. We can't get the county to adopt our major streets and land use plan.

What's wrong with this picture?

Are we experiencing growth pains or is there something seriously wrong here? Are we against progress at any cost? Are we willing to face the millennium with a plan, a direction, a means for all of us to progress and prosper? Are we willing to be controlled by those in the community who would be king; or those who continually subject us to their subjective objections ad nauseam; or those who conduct meetings in secrecy and display paranoiac behavior when asked about goings-on which concern the welfare of us all?

The San Miguel Basin Concerned Citizens Group has found a voice and direction. There's no question the rural segment needs to be heard and represented.

There's a small faction of the Concerned Citizens whose tactics at meetings leave much to be desired. Venting frustrations on members of boards and commissions will accomplish nothing other than galvanizing these same boards and commissions against them. People are more inclined to listen when they're not being bullied. These tactics belong in bars and alleys and not in meeting rooms where the serious business of community responsibility takes place.

If some of our more unruly country cousins took time to remember lessons most of us learned from our parents and grandparents, we might forego any more displays of embarrassing local behavior in public.

There are some Wright's Mesa residents who would have us believe they're for agriculture and preservation of long-standing tradition.

It ain't necessarily so. Development-minded ranchers are after zoning-free, fast and loose development opportunity. They're waging a water war with the town because water is the key to development.

Ag pretty much has its own way in the county and rightfully so. Our historical, cultural, social and economic structure is rooted in the rural and agricultural character of the San Miguel Basin. It is of paramount concern to everyone who lives here.

The county is growing at 11 percent annually. That's an alarming statistic. Telluride got to where it is today because it was fast and loose when there was money to be made. Decisions and deals were made in back rooms. There's a small group that made out like the bandits they are.

We need to control development to suit our needs. If we're to preserve the character of the area, which all sides seem to want on the surface, then we will need an economic base, which will work in conjunction with agriculture. Our own sawmill, milling our own lumber, employing our own people is a case in point. Forget the big outfits.

What we do now will set the tone for the quality of life for us, and our children, well into the 21st century. The San Miguel Basin is at stake. Let's not scare responsible employers and investors away with obstructionist attitudes.

It's time to clear away the smoke and mirrors and take a good hard look at what confronts us. Let the light shine on the issues. Let's make solid decisions based on fact and clarity.

Raymond Snyder Talks Water

Raymond Snyder has a firm grip on the big picture. He is a working rancher who has dealt with water and the lack of it his entire life in the San Miguel Basin, a former San Miguel County Commissioner, co-chair of the Dry Creek Basin Resource Management Committee and a member of the San Miguel Water Conservancy District.

Snyder described his view of the problems involving the Town of Norwood and the Norwood Water Commission with the rural sector, which extends past the limits of the town and into Montrose County.

The San Miguel Water Conservancy District, the Farmers Water Development Company and ranchers especially have been exasperated with the town's failure to live up to a merger contract, which combined the Norwood water system and the Wright's Mesa water system in the early 90's.

The two major points of contention are the raising of water tap rates and denial of rural commercial water taps outside the boundaries of the Norwood Plan.

"Both sides had to do certain things in that agreement," says Snyder. "There is a contract for the town to follow and they haven't been doing it.'

"We had to have a meeting when they arbitrarily decided to raise the rates for taps in the rural community. In the contract it says they can't do that. This contract is a public document between two public entities and anything to do with it has to be done in open, public discussion.

"Just a few months later they came up with this other issue.

184

They decided they could stop all commercial development outside the town's growth area. We tried to set up a meeting with the town. They met in executive session with three of our board members, Ivan McKinney, Dan Crane and Bill Bray. I wouldn't meet in executive session, neither would the rest of us. They were absolutely nasty to our people. At that point it developed into a stickier situation.

"We hired an attorney, started sending them letters and started negotiating with their attorney. They wouldn't acknowledge our attorney's letters for quite some time.

"They hired a new attorney and apparently she has advised them they couldn't win this lawsuit, that they will have to follow the contract. Their attorney has never told our attorney and the town has never told us, but the rumor I heard is June (Estep) put the word out that they are going to change their minds and reverse their decision, apparently due to the fact that it would involve them in a 5-year court case. She never officially notified anybody.

"There was a 3-3 tie on the Norwood Water Commission not to allow rural water taps. They went to the town board and made the decision. June's argument at the SMWCD meeting last week was that the town board was going to show courtesy to the water commission by letting them make the reversal decision. I believe that the town has to make the decision, put it on record that they have reversed their decision before it can go back to the water commission.

"We go from raising the rates, denial of commercial taps, and now they're setting up criteria for us to follow to appoint our rural members. Why can't these folks from the town follow the agreement and run this water commission without creating all these problems?

"We all know that the rural people and the town people can do this a lot better if they will just get together, stay together and run it together.

"It was set up this way years ago because the town couldn't get the money and the San Miguel Water Conservancy District, being a taxing entity, could get this rascal started. It helped the rural people and in turn helped the town people. But it's been a fight ever since because the town wants to be the authority on everything.

"We have to settle this thing without spending a lot of money and without a lot of conflict but we just flat haven't been able to do it. I asked June to make a statement announcing the reversal of their decision in the paper. She never did it.

"June runs this whole show, there's no question about it, along with Ralph Weaver and Marsha West. Everything is planned at their own little meetings and when it's put forth it's all cut and dried. The rural members were tired of getting run over roughshod. It brought things to a head and maybe sent a message that June's people are not the entire board, that they need rural people before they can proceed.

"I've been around this country too damned long not to see people work together, make a living and be happy in this community. I'd like to get this thing settled so we can all live together. I guarantee people used to work together until June came along and started raising so much hell. The Farmers Water people and the town had problems in the past but in the long run people went out and supported the town.

"If somebody wants a convenience store, a car wash or a bed and breakfast down in Redvale, they should be able to have it. If the water system was confined to the immediate area it wouldn't be so bad but this sucker runs clear down 15 miles west of Norwood and six or seven miles to the east.

"This is a planning issue and should be kept as planning. They shouldn't try to stifle development by using water."

"You can't believe how up in arms the rural people have been on account of that one damned decision by the town. Might not be but five commercial projects out of town in the next 20 years. The town is trying to cram it down their throats.

"The SMWCD can't sit on our butts and let this happen because it's a breach of contract in the agreement.

"I just want to get the facts straight on this issue. We have tried very, very hard to work this out with the town. They have showed us absolutely no courtesy at all.

"At a SMWCD meeting with June our entire board informed her we would not meet in executive session with the town over this because the contract is a public contract and they made the decision in a public meeting. We weren't going to discuss litigation unless the people could come listen in a public meeting. That way people would know what's going on. The town refused. Right after that meeting she went and posted the executive session meeting at the Post Office.

"When you start making decisions that are arbitrary and capricious, you're leaving yourself personally wide open for a lawsuit. I hate to see public entities get involved in lawsuits.

"I may have been a little rough on June at the SMWCD board meeting the other day when I called for her resignation. I want her to be aware if she tries to pull any of this crap she's pulled in town, she's going to be accountable for it. I thought I might as well let her know where I'm going to come from. The way this has all come about and the problems she's created, I very definitely feel that she has a strong conflict of interest.

"Conflict is created by people's actions. The things that June's pulled in the town, the way she's treated the SMWCD and the rural water people, have developed a strong conflict. If she'd been reasonable she wouldn't have such a strong conflict.

"I think it's really going to take June's getting realistic about some of these issues and concede the fact that, for the water alone, there's a contract the town has to follow and run the system equally with the rural people. They have to give the rural water commission an equal say in administering the system.

"They're going to have to set their differences and personality conflicts aside and run this sucker like a business. If June would ease up her attitude she'd be an excellent leader. You don't need to lead with arrogance. She needs to work with other people.

"I don't mind sitting on the board with June as long as she's fair and honest with us. She's done some good things for the town. She's worked hard, accomplished good things, gotten grants. But I really disagree with her getting these puppets together and doing everything herself.

"I just hope things level out and they quit abusing their authority so we all can work together."

Dean Stindt,
Conserving Resources

Dean Stindt considers his 16 years experience on the job and what he's learned from a lot of local ranchers a hell of a lot more important than the degree in natural resource management he earned from the University of Wisconsin.

Stindt works for the natural Resources Conservation Service, United States Department of Agriculture, in the San Miguel Basin. Despite the hefty governmental title, he's the most un-bureaucratic bureaucrat in southwestern Colorado.

Dean's job is to help ranchers and farmers conserve and develop their resources. He's a resource with access to resources to help local ag survive and thrive.

"For many years we were the Soil Conservation Service. Just recently we changed our name to the Natural Resources Conservation Service because there was a perception that all we did was work with farmers and ranchers on soil erosion problems. For years we've been doing much more than that. We work with all the resources. We deal with soil, water, plant, animal and human resource," says Stindt.

"We can't develop comprehensive, coordinated resource management plans without considering humans. I think we've gotten in trouble with that before. It's been suggested we eliminate timber sales in the Northwest to protect one species, the spotted owl. It was a one-dimensional approach to the problem. Maybe the human resource wasn't considered. It obviously had some impact on jobs for loggers in that part of the country. What our agency tried to look at are the impacts on all the resources, not just a single resource," Dean explains.

A lot of Stindt's time is spent in the field working with ranchers, farmers, landowners, archeologists and other governmental agencies to provide comprehensive resource management through technical assistance and hands-on help. When he's done in the field, he's in the office documenting the process.

Dean also helps by researching grants and providing financial assistance to individuals and committees.

"It's not a glamorous job. Too many times in government we don't have much to show for what we do. We do a hell of a lot of planning and a hell of a lot of discussing.

"Too many times nothing gets done on the land. I'm a firm believer in getting it done on the land. It's tough to work within the framework of government to get that done sometimes but that's where I get my real job satisfaction. I don't get all that much satisfaction writing an extensive plan on a piece of paper and then putting it on the shelf. The planning part of resource conservation in my mind is a means to an end. The next and most important step is to implement," he explains.

A major project Stindt has been working on is the agenda of the Dry Creek Basin Resource Management Committee.

"A lot of people, when they first saw us get going, thought we were just making more grass for the livestock. That just isn't true because the ranchers understand the importance of wildlife and clean water and the significance of cultural resources. This is a multiple resource plan. We're trying to address the full spectrum of resources in Dry Creek Basin. Any management action we take is going to be sensitive to all the resources. To be honest, that isn't how we've done things in the past. The CDOW can manage wildlife, the BLM manage for range habitat improvement, cultural resource people do what they need to do. We focus on soil and water conservation. We realize the inter-relationship and work together," Stindt explains.

"I'm excited about the prospect of everyone getting together and coming up with management action that makes a lot of sense from a watershed standpoint, a multiple resource standpoint. What I'm less than excited with is all the time and all the planning that has to go into it. There are a lot of people wanting to be involved in the management of public lands.

"Resources don't always follow governmental or institutional or property boundary lines. We define our planning unit in terms of the watershed area. We can't just say one group will manage private, one will manage BLM and one will manage CDOW. We're all involved in management decisions on the whole watershed. Cooperative effort is the way of the future.

"We're looking for more local involvement. To not tap into the pool of knowledge available from ranchers, people who have spent their entire lives on the land would be a major mistake. Probably 90% of what I know now about conservation and resource management in my day to day work I have learned from ranchers. They learned from being on the land and that's what I like to think my knowledge base is. Basically, everything I've learned is based on experience and I got that from the ranchers I work with.

"I've been working with this outfit since 1980 and I'm just now beginning to get comfortable with my experience base. I don't have the right answer all the time. I've worked with enough people who are on the land and have worked in the resource field, and that includes ranchers. You just can't stay in the ranching business unless you're a conservationist. Land, plants, wildlife, soil, water, people are resources that have to be managed in the right way or we'll lose them. We'll lose that productivity and any rancher I know realizes that fairly early. Ranchers have had to become conservationists.

"The San Miguel Basin Soil Conservation District is one of 80 districts in Colorado. This all began with the Dust Bowl in the 30's and the government got involved. That may have been a good idea in the 30's. There was a need for the federal government to come in and work with farmers and provide technical assistance to protect the soil and resources. Resource conservation problems are different and local conservation districts were created. The SMCBSCD includes all of San Miguel County and the western end of Montrose County. The district establishes priorities for resource concern in their purview. I am a USDA Natural Resource employee hired to assist in that. I provide them with technical assistance to implement the programs that they've devised or established in their area. The thing that's unique about our relationship with the conservation district is that kind of grass roots involvement. We do fairly well.

"The Natural Resources Conservation Service has survived and thrived, I believe, because we can say we're not big government jamming stuff down people's throats.

"Leslie Sherlock, June Estep, Cookie Been, the Weed Board, the Livestock Association and a lot of other good people, individual farmers and ranchers wrote letters in support of keeping this office here. It was a humbling experience for me. It showed me that maybe I was doing some good here after all.

"There's national interest in maintaining our country's ability and capability to provide food and fiber at a reasonable cost to the people. If we deplete our resources and don't manage them in a responsible way we basically lose that ability. In my opinion it is reversible. It takes a long time."

Rancher, Pilot, Neighbor

Derald Skalla Brings Perspective

Derald Skalla was born in the hospital in Telluride, in the building that now serves as the historical museum. He grew up in Norwood and Uravan and enlisted in the Navy in 1946 when he was 17.

The Navy sent Skalla to college and he became an officer, a fighter pilot and later a test pilot. After a naval career Skalla worked for Westinghouse in Baltimore, Maryland. Forty years after he left this area he returned with his wife Jan and son Matt and is a rancher in Redvale. He is also president of the board of the Farmers Water Development Company.

Derald decided to take early retirement and try his hand at ranching and farming rather than sit behind a desk. His spread sits not three miles from where Derald's grandparents had a farm.

Skalla agreed to an interview with The Post in an effort to get at the heart of the problems between the rural sector and the town of Norwood and communicate and clarify the position of the Farmers Water Development Company.

"It's hard to pinpoint where the problem started. When I was on the board and first moved back out here there was nothing but cooperation between the town and the ditch company," says Skalla. "The first or second year we moved out here the dam was being repaired. The reservoir had to be drained, there was very limited water for the summer and the ditch company actually put water in the Cone reservoir for the town's use. When the town ran out of water the shareholders always donated some of their own water. It was donated. It wasn't sold to the town.

"Exactly when the hostilities started I don't know. It may have started when they wanted to expand their water system and they had some ideas about using Gurley Reservoir at that time. One of the schemes was to put a new pipe through the dam. We said absolutely not. Even if we'd approved it, the state engineers would have disapproved it. Another scheme was to use our vent system and of course we were opposed to that. If anything had gone wrong with the vent system or the modifications, our only choice would have been to drain the reservoir. We didn't like them tampering with our vent system at all," Skalla recalls, "there were also other ideas which wouldn't have worked.

"So that may have been when the controversy started because it seemed everything they came up with, we opposed. There were valid reasons why we were opposed to each one of these items. At the time we were supplying winter water by having winter releases. We found out we couldn't release small amounts of water because it set up a cavitation problem with the headgate. The board decided they didn't want to fool with these winter water releases and the town had to do something to take care of their water supply in the winter without relying on our winter resources.

"Somewhere along the line they decided to build a reservoir instead. They could either build a reservoir or go to the river because they'd ruled out working with us.

"We had a couple of meetings with the Norwood Water Commission. At one of those meetings we got into a discussion about what caused the problem between the water commission and the ditch company. June Estep said she thought it started with that 'hostile letter.' What the letter stated was that at their present rate of use they'd run out of water by such and such date. This is a service not rendered to any other shareholder. I wish somebody would do that for me.

"I told June I thought the problem started when the water commission essentially started controlling the price of shares of Farmers Water Development Company by trading water taps for shares of water. That was done without any consultation whatsoever. They just did it and the next thing you know that was the policy. I think June did acknowledge, in a roundabout way, that they should have consulted with us before they did that. It resulted in the town controlling the price of our shares of water. A lot of shareholders were very upset about it. It inflated the price beyond agricultural use. It makes it so you can't afford to grow hay.

"That caused quite a bit of tension between the shareholders and the town. I don't know how many visits and phone calls I got from people who were upset.

"Attorney John Brooks convinced the water commission that we were going to have to augment the water we were supplying to the town, which was totally wrong. There were some people that were really upset about that because they could see us having to augment water we were supplying to the town. The way they saw it we were supplying water illegally to the town. This prompted us to take a close look at our decrees, which we did at a meeting with Ken Knox.

"It was a Norwood Water Commission meeting and our entire board attended that meeting. Ken Knox explained the decrees to the town and that's when it was made very clear what their sources of municipal water are. Knox put them up there and we knew they were all inactive or we were thoroughly convinced they were. Nobody said a word. The Norwood pipeline and infiltration system should probably be considered abandoned. They aren't producing any water. We went up and checked them and there's no evidence they're getting water from either one of those sources. That was their source of municipal water, made clear by Ken Knox.

"Another issue that really upset the rural community, which is most of the shareholders of Farmers Water Development Company is when they started discriminating against rural water users. First they put on the tap fees and it was half again as much for a rural tap as it was for a town tap. They finally backed off on that. That was definitely against the contract they signed. The other thing they came out with is no commercial taps in rural areas outside the town and Norwood expansion area. Now that really got a lot of shareholders upset. And they still are upset over this discrimination, which is actually against the contract signed with the San Miguel Water Conservancy when they took over the Wright's Mesa water system.

"So essentially, to me, that's where the hostility stems from. It may have started back on the controversy on the winter delivery of water and continued when they started trading taps for shares, and escalated with discrimination to rural users. That's what's got the rural water users upset and rightfully so.

"If someone wants to put in a convenience store in Redvale, they can't get a commercial tap. We can't get a commercial tap for anything. Some of the shareholders feel the town doesn't want industry coming into the rural areas. We don't have any industrial water anyway.

"Everything that we do is met with hostility by the Norwood Water Commission. The motivation behind our proposal on their big investment of building another reservoir was to save them half a million dollars. Three members of the water commission saw it as an attempt to shaft the town. What we set out to do was give them water at half the price it was going to cost them with a reservoir. That resulted in a profit to the ditch company and there's nothing wrong with that. The real intent of our proposal was to get the water at half price.

"What it comes down to is that our decrees do not allow for any municipal water. They cover irrigation, stock water, and the two most junior storage decrees and one of the free flowing decrees allows domestic use. Nobody ever made an issue of it before and we wouldn't make an issue of it now if they didn't have this discrimination policy against rural water users.

"We were going to guarantee them a minimum amount of water for domestic use. We never did guarantee them any water for municipal use. As I understand the distinction, domestic water is for household use and municipal water means use for public buildings, schools and parks.

"I even told them how to solve the problem. They have a quarter of a foot that they condemned in 1936 from one of our decrees. But when they condemned it they didn't change the use. The court order says 'the residents of Norwood and domestic purposes.' That should have been changed to municipal and industrial when they condemned it. They should look into changing that. Or maybe all that it would take is a ruling on what they mean by 'the residents of Norwood' in condemnation. That might be all it would take. That would be the first place to look for municipal water. They can't get it from our decrees.

"With a little bit of cooperation from the town we would be amenable not to press the issue. I would like to see things return to the cooperative basis we enjoyed when I first moved back here but under the current environment that's not going to happen because there's people on the board that are hostile towards Farmers Water Development Company."

Joe Vigil, Extraordinary Public Service

Joe Vigil's got a list of public service accomplishments longer than the combined curl of his signature moustaches. He's been a pharmacist and major league contributing member of the San Miguel Basin community for 35 years. He's been Santa Claus in the area for over 30 years for Elk and Moose Lodges, veteran's organizations, churches and schools.

Joe's always good for a smile on the street or in his pharmacy. He's available to give a helping hand whether you're a veteran or a kid or somebody in need.

Last year Joe was Colorado's Elk of the Year. He was initiated into the BPOE in 1965 and served as Telluride's Golden Antler Exalted Ruler in 1974-75, State Association Tiler, Trustee, Chaplain, Americanism Chairman and Drug Abuse Chairman.

Vigil was elected mayor of Norwood in 1980 and served on the Town Board of Trustees. Joe's been a member of the Regional 10 Board, Regional Planning Commission, Member's Finance Committee of Region 10, Colorado Municipal League and Energy Impact Committee for San Miguel County.

Vigil graduated in Pharmacy in 1946, earned a BS/BA from the University of Denver in 1953, an MBA from the University of Denver in 1954, continued his graduate studies at Colorado University in 1968, 1970, 1972-75, 1977. He got a Pharmacy Doctor's degree in 1982.

The list goes on: Joe was appointed to the first Governor's Conference on Health Planning in 1978, served as president of the Western Slope Pharmaceutical Association for three years and as a member for 30 years, been a registered pharmacist in Colorado since 1946, member of the Board of Directors for Western Colorado Health Systems Agency for 12 years, member of the American Health Planning Association, Health Officer of the Western Colorado Boy Scout Ranch for three years, pharmaceutical consultant for Norwood Emergency Clinic for 15 years, member of the Norwood Volunteer Fire Department and Ambulance for three years, chairman for the March of Dimes campaign for San Miguel and Montrose Counties for three years.

Vigil is a 32nd Degree Mason, worked with the Boy Scouts of America for over 30 years, been a member of the Norwood Lions Club for five years and the Nucla Moose Lodge for 18 years. He's on the Veteran's Remembrance Committee and places flags on veterans' and Elks' graves in Norwood Cemetery on Veterans and Memorial Days.

The list goes on and on and on. You've got the idea. Joe takes participation and community seriously.

Vigil is married to wife Eunice. They have two sons, five daughters, two sons-in-law, 13 grandchildren and seven great-grandchildren.

Joe was born in Trinidad, Colorado, where his father was a cop, Joe's dad had a friend who was fairly high up in an organization called the "Black Hand," a sort of Mafia in Eastern Colorado in its day. The "friend" became Joe's kid brother's godfather to get Joe's dad in his back pocket. Joe's father decided to move the family to Denver rather than be beholding to the mob.

Joe's dad got a job on the railroad in Denver because of "the pension" to provide for his family. He also worked at the Albany and Savoy Hotels as a second cook to the chef until World War I and the Depression were over. The chef always sent leftovers home for the kids.

"I never ate oatmeal until after the war," says Joe, who sold newspapers on the corner when he was a kid to help out his family.

He graduated from Denver's West High School. "I must have had too much fun in high school because I stayed for five years. I was short a couple courses and instead of graduating in January I graduated in June."

Joe got a summer job after high school working in the Stanley Hotel kitchen as a dishwasher. He worked his way up to pantryman. The chef wanted Joe to stick with cooking, promising he'd make Joe a chef. Joe stayed at the hotel. Eventually Joe and the chef had a disagreement. The chef, who stood 6'4" tall and weighed 360lbs, drank a quart of bourbon a day.

"The chef got crotchety and I got crotchety right back. That was the end of that," says Joe.

Joe became a machinists apprentice and later enlisted in the service. After basic training Joe was offered OCS or the Army specialized training program.

"They were willing to put people with potential in college," Joe explains. "They were going to send me to the University of Wyoming. We missed the train and were sent to the South Dakota School of Mines instead. I met my wife Eunice there. Shortly after we got there they decide to disband the school. I transferred into the Air Force. They shipped me to St. Louis and after that it was San Antonio for basic, Midland for bombardier training and Laredo, Texas, for gunnery training."

After the service Joe took his credits and GI Bill and went to pharmacy school. He took a job as a pharmacist. He also worked as a cab driver at night and went to school in the day and started a dry cleaning business. The cleaning fumes started to bother Joe and eventually he and his family moved out of Denver to State Bridge, Colorado, where they ran a small resort eatery on the Colorado River. The business wasn't making money so the family moved ten miles up the river to a ranch in Radium. The Colorado Department of Wildlife offered Joe the ranch for $1 a year rent.

"My kids all said that was the happiest time in their lives," says Joe Vigil.

The train went right by their place and all the engineers and trainmen knew Joe's kids. The kids would shine flashlights at the trains at night. The train stopped to take Joe's daughter to school in Bond.

A minister friend of Joe's brother talked Joe into taking a pharmacist's job in Uravan. The kids rebelled at first and threatened to move in with grandpa in Denver but finally relented.

"We decide to give it a try. The kids were good sports," says Joe.

Eventually Joe and the family bought a house on 40 acres in Nucla. Joe commuted until the kids put up Christmas lights, overloaded the circuits and the house burned down.

Joe was offered the pharmacy in Norwood by a friendly

business rival. He gave his employer in Uravan a month's notice and took the offer.

"Here we are," says Joe, "we've been here ever since. That's pretty close to 35 years. Frank Wilson tried to sell me the pharmacy in Telluride for $25,000. That was lock, stock and barrel and included a gallon of tincture of heroin."

"An economic development guy out of Grand Junction came by with a plan to help us build this new store and we did it about 20 years ago," Joe explains.

"That's how we ended up here and from there on it's been a wonderful life. I couldn't have done it without my lovely, understanding and patient wife Eunice. She's got a great sense of humor," says Joe.

"Never pick a fight with someone who buys ink by the barrel." -Mark Twain

COMMENTARY&OPINION

The San Miguel County Post 1/17/96

Thoughts On Regional Transportation

In the course of this past week I had occasion to attend several meetings but one stuck in my mind as exemplary of the difference in attitudes between the East and West Ends of San Miguel County.

First I had the pleasure of attending the Vision 2020 meeting in Telluride dealing with their evolving regional transportation plan. I welcome such far-reaching ideas but when plan presenter Jim Burleigh made a statement to the effect that the plan doesn't necessarily fit the boundaries of the county, I grew immediately suspicious.

Burleigh, as well as a majority of those luminary land owners, developers, planners, visionaries, county commissioners and town council persons agreed that the regional plan was geared more toward Montrose than the West End.

This surprised me, since the highway from Norwood to Placerville is congested with traffic that is generated by development in Telluride with a work force without which Telluride, most probably, would not exist.

And those residents don't need Telluride's precious "low cost" housing, which isn't so low cost after all and denigrates the people who live there into second-class citizens who can't get along without government assistance.

Take, for example, the personnel who work for Ray Hughes in the maintenance department. His work force commutes daily from Norwood. Where would Telluride be without a maintenance crew to haul off the snow, clean the public toilets, sand the streets, keep the water running, make sure the sewage flows downhill and put up all those infernal signs?

Several of the attendees spoke in lofty, albeit smoky terms about transportation other than "rubber wheeled." Trucks run on rubber tires, planes land on rubber tires, bicycles use rubber tires. The talk about gondolas and transportation corridors induced me to think that the Klingons were about to land and we were all going to get teleported to who knows where.

When I asked Burleigh about how the "regional" plan affects Norwood and the West End, I was treated to an explanation about how people in Egnar think that Burleigh and the people in Telluride are weird. You are weird, Jim. Ask anybody with a smidgeon of common sense.

The consensus was that Norwood needs to be "serviced." I was really getting nervous now. Are we waiting for THEM to land and teach us how to teleport so we don't need to use rubber tires?

When Burleigh spoke of "caveat" I was hoping that they'd break out the crackers and heap on the fish eggs. No such luck. Things in Telluride aren't all that great just yet.

"Caveat", according to Webster, is "a warning enjoining one from certain acts or practices." This term derives from the Latin "caveat emptor", which means "Let the buyer beware." Indeed.

I'm for an ACTUAL regional transportation plan, which includes EVERYBODY in the region. I think Vision 2020 needs to get to the drawing board and not let the plan out of the bag until they have a solid idea of what it is they want. Intercept parking and gondolas be damned! Let's put some pressure on the state to improve the highway or build a new one from Dallas Divide, over Hastings Mesa, along Last Dollar Road—what an appropriate name!

The Open Space Commission meeting, which was also held in Telluride, had Marty Zeller, a Denver consultant and regional planner hired by the commission on a GOCO grant to identify options to keep land open in the West End.

His presentation was terse, to the point and enlightening. He had conducted group discussions with more than 30 West End residents concerning their interests in open space preservation techniques.

What he discovered was that more than space and distance separates East from West. He found completely different cultures, completely different attitudes toward land use, two different economic bases, in essence—two different counties.

What is wrong, Zeller discerned, is that there is loss of trust and substantial skepticism in the West End as it regards the general feeling that the county commissioners aren't interested in issues important to this end of the county but are embroiled in high-dollar development stakes and political correctness standards of a culture which has very little to do with the reality of life in the West End.

He concluded that there is an opportunity here for the commissioners to respond realistically and resolve an antagonistic situation by preserving a more diverse community with actual affordable housing and flexible land uses based on a good neighbor performance policy. Makes sense.

Another option is to reinstate the notion that there ARE two different counties and finally do something about it. Amen.

Onerous Regulations

After two years and 21 meetings the net result of what is euphemistically known as the Logging Task Force is that it's a total farce. It would have been better to name it The Recreational Use Task Force or the Let's Stamp Out Logging Task Force or The Bambi Eco-Warrior's Guide to County Politics.

Art Goodtimes, much to his credit, has done a capable job of trying to keep opposing factions at bay, despite the fact that he remains less than objective and keeps the balance of the farce tilted towards eco-sensitivity.

Where Art and his cohorts came up with the knowledge to negate the findings, systems and data of both state and federal forest service representatives is beyond me. The foresters have spent decades studying how to ensure the abundance and survival of the forest and how to allow forest use for all of us on an equal basis.

What it seems Art and his cohorts at the county planning office and the county attorney's office and at least one member of the BOCC have wrought is pending legislation designed to choke off and kill logging in San Miguel County.

"Onerous" is the word Art used to describe the "Good Logging Practices" process about to be handed to the county planning commission and the board of county commissioners.

"Onerous", according to Webster, means "Involving, imposing or constituting a burden, having legal obligations that outweigh the advantages."

It seems the county and the eco-conspiracy are out to nag people wanting to make a fair living in the forest to death with more restrictive and non-flexible legislation.

Then, "The Farce" recommends creating a Logging Enforcement Officer. Who is going to pay for this neo-ecocop? We are. Do we actually need more cops in the county? It all depends on your point of view. Used to be you went about your business here and unless you were abusing the overall good you got left alone.

When I asked Art if skidding logs in winter is good logging practice, he squirmed and wriggled but wouldn't give me a straight answer. The best he could do is say "it is a more complex issue involving recreation."

I could hear the shrews, shrikes and banshees of Wright's Mesa shrieking in the back of Art's eco-consciousness.

What this issue comes down to is that snowmobilers want to run wild all over the county in winter without regard to the fact that there are loggers who want to work to support their families.

Then there's the issue of private property rights. If the county can tell loggers how to log on private property, then they can tell ranchers how to graze and farmers how to farm and how to transport over county roads which, by the way, are public.

The county seems intent on killing off an industry that helped build it. Without wafer board, 2x4's and logs, the building boom Telluride is enjoying wouldn't be possible. Is it better to import wood from other states?

Doug Wakefield wasn't kidding when he said "Logging in this county is OK if you log in some other county and bring the wood in."

Can we afford to lose more industry when what we need is economic diversity to survive? Can we afford to lose the use of renewable resources we all depend on? Can we allow county government to regulate us ad nauseam according to the dictates of current political correctness?

The San Miguel County Post 7/17/96

Water Cooperation

On the surface, water seems to be the major controversial issue in the West End and the San Miguel County Basin.

Below the surface, the water issue becomes the focus in a struggle for control, dominance and influence on Wright's Mesa.

Water is the key to controlling development. Development is the key to economic growth and sustainability in this western end of the basin.

For generations, the Good 'Ol Boy system worked just fine in this end of the county and beyond. There was no clear difference between Norwood town residents and Wright's Mesa residents. We were all neighbors and helped each other out when there was need.

The ranchers and major landowners took care of the water and everybody got along fine. The San Miguel Water Conservancy District did its job, as did the Farmers Water Development Company. The status quo was maintained and there was, relatively speaking, peace in the valley.

As long as everybody was part of the Good 'Ol Boy system, everything was fine. Then New Telluride happened and the people started moving in and the problems started, as far as the Good 'Ol Boys are concerned.

The dilapidated old water system, which had adequately served for decades, was no longer adequate. Baling wire and hope would no longer work. Something had to be done so the town took over the Wright's Mesa water system. The townies and the rurals struck a deal and everything was going to be hunky dory. It didn't quite turn out that way.

The mayor decided that the Good 'Ol Boy system wasn't quite fair if you weren't a Good 'Ol Boy. She wanted a system where everybody got treated the same according to the laws and regulations of all the citizens. She wasn't a Good 'Ol Boy. She was part of the New Wave that was rocking the system.

The mayor had a vision of a town with its own future, with a light industrial zone so that the local citizens could be gainfully employed without having to depend entirely on Telluride for their economic well being. She realized that not everyone in the area could work as a rancher or a cowboy. Mining in the area was all but history. We needed jobs that could put our citizens and kids to work and keep the local energy and smarts at home. She set to fixing the streets, planting trees and flowers, renovating Town Hall, building a new reservoir, fixing the water system.

The mayor's vision is a great one. She's a smart, tough and incredibly energetic person. She's so good at what she does that nobody ran against her and she's mayor by acclamation.

Sixty-five western economists back the mayor up. A recent study issued by the economists says that below-cast timber sales, subsidized water for ranching and farming and hard-rock mineral giveaways on federal land herald the decline of resource-based economics of the Old West. Legislators and economists agree that protecting ranching and logging as a way of life is a cultural argument.

There's no argument that the mayor has done a great job. What she hasn't done is treat the rural people fairly. She apparently hasn't stuck to the deal made with the rural sector as far as commercial water taps and raising tap fees.

The town can't dictate to the outlying areas what's what. It ain't necessarily so. The actual Good 'Ol Boys haven't been dictated to in over a hundred years in this area and you can bet your boots they're not about to start.

The mayor needs to stick to the deal and deal with the rural people with respect. We don't need more social, economic or cultural fracturing in the area. What we need is to work on our problems together like the neighbors and good Westerners we are. There's nothing we can do about Telluride but there's something we can do about our own back yard.

It can only work if the Good 'Ol Boys give the mayor a hand rather than try to sabotage her at every turn. Respect has to be mutual in order to work. It takes two to tango and good will on both sides.

Neighborhood of Strangers

There is a giant ray of hope on the horizon. The Town of Norwood Trustees, the Norwood Water Commission and the San Miguel Water Conservancy District will meet publicly to discuss pertinent and controversial issues regarding water service to Wright's Mesa including Norwood on Tuesday, July 23, 7:30pm at the Norwood Community Center.

Be there and bring your good neighbor attitude. You get what you give.

Extending Town Boundaries

It wasn't all that long ago that a person's word was their bond around here. A handshake sealed the deal. You stuck to the deal you made because that was the honorable thing to do. Unfortunately that era is over.

Witness the water entities' meeting at the community center. June Estep, Norwood mayor, Norwood Water Commission member, Norwood Town Trustee, San Miguel Water Conservancy District director, brought her lawyers to a meeting where we were going to get things out in the open and begin to discuss them. What were the lawyers for?

The mayor partially explained her intent, while trying yet another circuitous explanation why she isn't following the contract made between the town and mesa residents.

"Things are not as cut and dried, even in contracts, as they appear to be," Estep stated.

The reason you bring a lawyer in to explain why you're not keeping your end of the bargain is because you're apparently trying to weasel out of the deal.

Estep went to a lot of trouble to draft new rules of conduct for Norwood Water Commission members because rural appointee M.J. Cadgene didn't agree with the mayor's goals, aspirations or tactics. M.J. was a constant burr under the mayor's saddle. Cadgene is off the commission and the mayor gets her way once again. The problem with this is that the mayor is now attempting to dictate to the SMWCD criteria for rural members of the NWC. If Cadgene was guilty of conflict of interest, then the mayor best resign from some of the boards she's on because she faces a more complex and intense dilemma.

The town board approved allowing commercial water taps outside the Norwood Urban Growth Boundary at their May 14 meeting. They approved the resolution after discussing the proposition in executive session, which may not be legal under Colorado's Sunshine Law.

Then the water commission drafted two resolutions, #0723 and #0724, which place contingencies on issuance of water taps.

#0724 states that before any water tap is issued "The Commission shall be reactionary to the land use planning efforts and processes of local government. Toward that end, evidence of compliance with all applicable governmental zoning, and land use regulations; evidence of consistency with the applicable Comprehensive or Master Plan, and evidence that all necessary approvals have been obtained, shall be required prior to or as a condition of the issuance of any water tap."

At the last water commission meeting I asked Marsha West why the commission felt it necessary to place such contingencies on water tap issuance. She answered with concern about the quality of developments on the mesa.

The business of the Norwood Water Commission is to sell taps and deliver water. It's none of their business what people do or don't do on the mesa. The authority of the Norwood Town Board ends at the boundaries of the town. The commission and the board are essentially one and the same. June Estep, Ralph Weaver and Marsha West vote in a bloc and have for some time. There may be some truth to the fact that the mayor and her cohorts allegedly discuss business at the mayor's kitchen table, which should be discussed in open public meetings. These discussions may not be entirely legal under Colorado's Sunshine Law.

There is an apparent parallel between the mayors of Telluride and Norwood. Neither respects the rights or wishes of people outside their town boundaries. They have displayed tendencies to cram unpopular and unsolicited regulations, resolutions, possibilities and influences down the throats of people who will no longer accept such outrageous, unacceptable behavior.

The mayor's lawyers are costing us money, which we pay in monthly fees. The price of water is going up. The last increase was 33%, despite the shuck and jive the mayor hands us. The price of water has gone up 60% in the last two years. There have been no new taps sold to fund Estep's Folly. We're in deep trouble with the mayor's ambitions, which are continually raising the cost of living in our working class community.

If the mayor didn't get the message last Tuesday, maybe she'd better get a grip. The rural people are extremely pissed off. There are people in town who feel the same way. Up front neighborly honesty, not lawyers and smoke, will go a long way to sorting things out and getting them back on the right track.

The words of the town government and water commission apparently aren't worth the hot air they're made with. The mayor and her flunkies need to be watched closely. Have a lawyer check any agreement you may have made with the town or water commission. This is going to an expensive proposition. The Estep Era is upon us.

The San Miguel County Post 7/7/96

Getting All The People Together

After visiting with neighbors and friends in town and out, I get the impression that most of the people on Wright's Mesa, which includes the Town of Norwood, not the other way around, have had enough of the mayor of Norwood, her boards, commissions and lawyers, and want to take positive steps to clarify and remedy the situation.

People are concerned about how we're going to pay off the nearly $2 million debt incurred by the Norwood Water Commission. People on the mesa pay a majority of the water bills but have virtually no say in how the system is run. This is a situation that needs to be addressed immediately.

The mayor is trying to force flagpole annexation on people potentially affected by and adamantly opposed to such a move. If the mayor gets quit claim deeds to the rights-of-way from the county, in three years she'll be able to annex properties affected without the voters' approval. She tries to control planning and zoning outside Norwood through water.

We've already got county commissioners and P&Z who are unresponsive to our needs and wishes. We don't need another government to tell us what to do or how to do it. We need responsive, independent, clear thinking individuals who will listen to what we need and want and represent us accurately.

The mesa and town have historically been one community. It seems the mayor and her cronies have been working overtime to change that. There's just too much power in the hands of three people who directly affect a much larger community than they legally represent. A politically apathetic community in Norwood has helped them get away with it.

ALL OF THE PEOPLE involved need to have a say in what affects their lives and economy. We're still one community, the town and the mesa, no matter what the mayor's boards and commissions are up to.

Let's have a Mesa Meeting with ALL OF THE PEOPLE: townies, rurals, business folks, children, cowboys, ranchers, commissioners, sheriffs, mayors, board and commission members but NO LAWYERS!

This time we meet in the San Miguel Basin Arena and not the mayor's community center. Let's make this a country affair where we can all breathe. We need just one impartial moderator to run the whole deal, someone who is respected and will be minded by everybody. We need a specific agenda and a question and answer period where ALL OF THE PEOPLE can be heard.

Let us act like the good neighbors we are, who treat each other the way we want to be treated. Let us find out where we stand and what needs to be done. We need ALL OF THE PEOPLE all of the time. Let's make it work.

Kitchen Cabinet

"We have met the enemy and they is us," Pogo was fond of saying in a comic strip full of swamp characters a few years back. Seems to me what Pogo said applies to us on Wright's Mesa today.

There's been a lot of finger pointing and blaming going on around here lately. The ranchers blame the mayor. The mayor blames the ranchers. They blame us, we blame them, Pogo was right.

Nobody ran against the mayor for her second term. She became mayor by acclamation because she was the only one who wanted it. She conducts her business the best way she knows how. June Estep is good at what she does. She's so good that she's got the entire mesa wondering of we're us or we're them.

The mayor's "Kitchen Cabinet" would have us believe that their motives are entirely altruistic. Not so. The same holds true of her opposition. Everybody involved has ulterior motives that they're not willing to share publicly.

As far as the town is concerned, the people on Wright's Mesa can take a flying leap in a rolling doughnut. The people on the mesa still have the right to develop as they see fit, if this is still America and not some cheap shot Third World dictatorship. Besides, dealing with county P&Z is something only a self-styled masochist would take on.

A scenario I encountered in Telluride lately to solve West End woes involves Norwood discorporating, and a mesa-wide metro district being established. Everybody'd have a vote. We wouldn't have to pay extra for police. The county would have to maintain all the roads. Sounds good to me, possibly better than seceding from the county or blowing up the Norwood Bridge. How would we get to work?

San Miguel County is a misnomer. In reality it's Telluride

County; they generate the money, call the shots. The 145 spur into Telluride is already known as the "Little Hollywood Freeway."

One of the major factors in this latter-day tragedy is that it's a foregone conclusion that we've been signed, sealed and delivered to high-dollar development interests. It's also a foregone conclusion that ranching, logging and mining are occupations whose time is past.

Property taxes are going up, the price of water is going up, the price of real estate is going up, the price of services are up. When that happens, the working family and people on fixed incomes have to move on. Ridiculously priced "affordable housing" appears. Look at Telluride. Realty and development interests move in and take over. There is a Telluride realtor on both the water commission and the town board.

When money talks, real values are silenced, gentrification happens and the reason you and I live here evaporates. The view remains for the realtors to exploit. When money talks, what it usually says to working people is goodbye.

We have met the enemy and they is us.

The San Miguel County Post 7/21/96

Norwood Ambition

How do we recall a mayor we didn't elect?

We could politely ask her to resign and retire to her ranch in Montrose County. She might sell her holdings in and around Norwood and be appointed a rural member of the Norwood Water Commission. If that doesn't work, we can get together a petition with 15% of the people who actually elected her and get the process started.

We don't need the mayor's vision or the industrial zone or an inflexible, unchangeable master plan. What we need first is our entire community back. Since it's obvious that the county commissioners don't listen to what the people in the West End say or want, we need to get our own house in order and get local government to represent what the majority of the people in the area do want. Then we can see about the rest.

It's apparent that people on Wright's Mesa want to be left alone. The real vocal minority in this area is the mayor and her sanctimonious flunkies. Take away the Zehm and Grimes properties in the proposed industrial zone and there's virtually nobody to support the mayor out there. Zehm and Grimes both live elsewhere. The citizens who've lived here for decades want the residential neighborhoods they raised their families in, not an industrial zone. People on Wright's Mesa don't trust June Estep with good reason.

There was a county P&Z meeting in Telluride last week dealing with flagpole annexation outside Norwood. That's right, neighbors, they had it up in Telluride in the middle of the day. The Miramonte Room was packed and overflowed into the halls. Dozens of working people who want to preserve their residential way of life explained to the commission that they do not want the mayor's plan.

The commission voted in favor of quit-claiming the county roads to the Town of Norwood despite the overwhelming, valid protests and thus began the process of flagpole annexation. It goes to the commissioners next. My prediction is that Anna Zivian will make a motion to approve, Craft will second. Zivian will vote for, Craft will follow and Leslie Sherlock will vote against. Same old vote, same old story, same old deal. Telluride controls our local politics. There's no need to go to Telluride. They don't care what we want and they refuse to listen.

June Estep publicly kissed the butts of Zivian and Craft and the Telluride contingent of county P&Z in Telluride's Daily Planet last week, begging them to approve her flagpole annexation. It worked. She kissed up fine. It doesn't matter what the people want. It does matter whose butt you kiss.

Marsh West showed her true colors at the P&Z meeting when she doffed her "ethical" hats as a government representative and spoke up for her clients as the real estate hustler she actually is. Ms. West, the mayor's head flunkie, has a major league conflict of interest but refuses to acknowledge it.

Richard Grice, who parades as Norwood's town planner, an Estep hire, used David Lavender's description of Norwood as a "ramshackle little town with unpainted houses with shutters hanging down," as an accurate portrait of Norwood today. His statement is an insult to the people of Norwood, Wright's Mesa and the entire West End. I offered to interview him in the elevator but he graciously declined. He is an arrogant person who's been run out of both Aspen and Telluride. Health reasons should prevent him from coming to Norwood.

The mayor's legacy to this community is dissent, disruption, discontent and a debt we'll have to pay for decades. Let her plant her trees in her own garden. Once she's out of here we can get back to living in a community where every voice counts.

Turning Point

It wasn't until I signed the papers on 1360 Cedar Street, Norwood, Colorado, that I began to see the light. I realized I was committed to the proposition that a person can live a rural lifestyle with reasonable people in a reasonable neighborhood with some of the most awesome views in the world.

Little did I realize that there was a movement afoot dedicated to destroying my vision and peace of mind by catering to an onslaught of urban expectations and a developmental gravy train. I based my lifestyle hopes on the down-home realistic values of friends and neighbors I have cultivated over more than two decades. Norwood seemed to me to be a dream worth pursuing. This is not an economic opportunity for me. This is my home.

For months I backed the mayor without question. I wrote an editorial, which was printed in the Telluride Times Journal taking ranchers and agricultural types to task for being obstructionists. At the same time I helped the Concerned Citizens find their voice. I believe everybody has a right to be heard. There are a lot of things I may be guilty of but being unprofessional isn't one of them.

I believe that all people have a right to determine what they-want. I respect my neighbor's wishes and opinions. I expect them to respect mine. When I make a deal I keep it. After 51 years I'm more convinced than ever that a person's word is their most important asset.

One of my favorite guys, Thomas Jefferson, said: "Were it left for me to decide whether we should have a government without newspapers or newspapers with a government, I should not hesitate a moment to prefer the latter."

For quite a while I believed the mayor and then discovered that she hadn't been entirely truthful. None of the ranchers would talk with me when I was privy to the mayor's kitchen. It made me curious why so I made an attempt to open a dialogue.

It turns out that the people outside Norwood have a point of view, which is a lot closer to mine than the mayor's. We all see this as a great place to live. We still trust in the ability of all the people to make sound decisions on their own. There are generations of tradition and values at stake here.

In my opinion, the mayor and her Kitchen Cabinet are ripping the heart and soul out of Wright's Mesa, planning for the big bucks, waiting for the gravy train, looking out for their own best interests under the guise of responsible development.

I'm out there trying to rip up the tracks because I don't want to get any on me. This is where I draw the line, where I make my stand.

Last Friday I called the mayor and offered to interview her so she could tell all the people what she's up to and why. She wanted time to think about it and said she'd get back to me. So far she hasn't called.

Expensive Proposition

There must be a reason why Norwood is politically apathetic. I couldn't come up with one so I decided to ask friends and neighbors what they think the reason is.

Two theories emerged. The first assumes that since television takes up a majority of the residents' leisure time, no time is available to interact, gossip over the fence or discuss events of political import. It's easier to turn on the tube rather than attend a meeting after work.

The second theory is based on the trust of neighbors who have known each other all their lives, who assume that whoever is in office is doing a good job because they're a neighbor and therefore trustworthy.

For decades the politics of this town was run on this assumption. Unfortunately this rural, neighborly political policy is no longer viable. With the influx of people from 'the real world', we're having to deal with 'real world' politics.

Now we need to bring a lawyer to public meetings to decipher what the mayor's lawyer is saying. We are in danger of losing the ability to communicate directly, person to person, neighbor to neighbor, friend to friend. It is not only a dangerous, but an expensive situation.

So far this year our mayor has spent $19,818.22 in lawyer's fees. She's spending your money. $14,273.38 was paid to attorney Janice Sheftel for the Singletree litigation, $3,602.84 was paid to attorney Sherry Caolia for water rights and commercial taps and $1,942.00 was paid to attorney Eric Heil for town board advice.

Our mayor has spent nearly $30,000 in attorneys' fees over the last three years on the Singletree litigation alone. These are not figures I made up to embarrass her honor but I asked at the town hall and was presented with these fiscal facts by the town clerk. Why hasn't the town been publishing its bills in the local paper? The Norwood Water Commission has an excuse because they're not an elected public board and are not required by law to do so.

Why does a town of 450 people need so many lawyers? Why does the mayor feel the need to bring her lawyers to nearly every public meeting? Is this the price of progress?

At the last Norwood Water Commission meeting most of the questions were addressed to the commission's lawyer. Who is running the show here? Fortunately for all of us Don Erickson asked what she was doing here, why she was here and who authorized her to be here. Hopefully, future meetings will be more reasonable with board and commission members able to discuss issues, problems and solutions without expensive interference. There have been questions raised by the public as to who is coming up with our ideas and resolutions and why. So far no answers have been provided.

As concerns the issue of trust, public or otherwise, consider the fact that at the last San Miguel Water Conservancy Board of directors meeting June Estep and Marsha West both insisted that the NWC had sold taps this year. At the NWC meeting, Estep and West were both asked the same question and asked to provide the names of the people to whom the taps had been sold. They relented and admitted that they are confused. I'm not accusing them of anything. You decide for yourself what is and what's not. Perhaps the job is too taxing for our mayor and her realtor buddy and they should take a break. Being confused about no taps being sold this year may just be the tip of the iceberg. The mayor apologized about not putting the rural water tap issue on the agenda because she forgot, pretty convenient, being confused and forgetting.

I checked Town Hall records and no taps had been sold this year. 13 taps, all rural, had been sold in 1995. A total of 31 taps have been sold and are not yet serviced. The money for these taps has apparently been spent.

The mayor's cooperation is certainly appreciated, as is Marsha West's and Ralph Weaver's in working with the new rural members of the NWC in coming to unanimous decisions at the last meeting. A public work session dealing with poignant and controversial issues is certainly a step in the right direction. Could this be a new era of communication and trust? It's still too early to tell and I'd keep a lawyer on retainer before we jump for joy and reassume the couch of our former politically apathetic state.

There is still a BOCC public hearing on flagpole annexation coming up in Norwood, October 2, 7:00pm. Ask your neighbors what they think, how they feel, what they want. Tell them what you want. Let's open the dialogue and tell the commissioners how we feel.

In the meantime, we still need to keep an eye on the mayor. People don't change overnight. My invitation to the mayor still stands. So far, she hasn't called.

This Is Post Country

Consider the nature of Post Country, the nature of people the San Miguel County Post represents. We represent the peripheral view, the minority, the working class heroes, the ranchers, the farmers, the ag types, the loggers, the service folks, what's left of the miners, what's left of the heart and soul of the county.

In my opinion we represent the reasonable view, the view of those actually concerned with taking care of the land on a day to day basis, as compared to the most densely populated, most offensive as far as the amount of pollution it generates, outrageously overbearing, confused part of the county, the county seat, Telluride.

Telluride keeps adding more and more population to the county while screaming its danged fool head off about 'environmental' concerns. Who keeps adding yummy effluent to the San Miguel River, compiled of the rapidly growing sewage in town and all the continually increasing developments surrounding it? Who keeps complaining about the traffic caused by all the development? Who wants to shut down logging as they build trophy log homes and stick-built condo bondage semi-Victorian, neo-Tyrolean, Disney-like buildings? Why does it look like L.A. on killer smog alert when you drive into town in the morning? Who can afford a deed-restricted $250,000 home unless it's part of some scam? Who needs it? Why is this insanity being perpetrated on all of us in the name of economic development and responsible growth? Have all you people lost your minds totally or is this some kind of insane hoax?

Friends who still live in Telluride or it's burbs complain that there's too much news coverage. There are too many papers covering too much stuff and not saying anything, old timers say. My friends insist that if the papers actually reported what's happening rather than insist that there's something going on every second, there'd only be a newspaper printed once a month or so. In fact, they'd like to see a newspaper void of malarkey, exclaiming that there is no news today. Now a paper runs on its advertising and perhaps we'd all be better off by saying that the only reason we're in business is because we can make a living by selling. KOTO already supplies the news for free and you don't need to be able to read to get it either. And you can get NPR propaganda as icing on the illiteracy cake. This is the best of all worlds. Most of my friends still lost in non-Post Country have stopped reading the papers altogether in an effort to improve their day.

It seems exceedingly strange that the Democratic candidate whom the county voters have chosen to represent the West End, euphemistically known as the 3rd District, neither represents or is of the West End. He lives on the outskirts of Norwood with his family in an abode so aptly described by Norwood Town Planner Richard Grice at the last county planning commission meeting. He hustles his shuck and jive street theater dance routine totally in Telluride. This guy is an amazing performer, a self-proclaimed poet who possesses an uncanny ability to talk out of both sides of his mouth at the same time, with an equally uncanny ability to convince both sides he's representing them since they're both undoubtedly right. He operates with a fondness for truth, which rivals Jimmy Swaggart's. This is a guy Telluride deserves and is willing to vote for. He's a real politician's politician who's looking for a county commissioner's ride since self-proclaimed poetry doesn't pay very well. If Craft can do it why shouldn't he?

Now readers in Post Country aren't quite as easy to fool. They work for a living, for one thing. And they're certain that they have to pay for what they get. And they've got a real, truth speaking, down home, fourth generation, rancher businessman Republican candidate in Jim Young. Jim won't dazzle you with horse pucky, mirrors and smoke but will tell you what he actually thinks. He believes in the land and the people and how hard we all have to work to keep what we've got to keep going. He's not about to make any deals until he's assured that everyone will make out.

Post Country won't change anytime soon. We'll still represent the reasonable view. I'm certain there are folks who will disagree, more power to them. I don't attempt to tell readers what they should think or do. That's something they'll have to do for themselves. I try to call it as close to the bone as I can. The rest is a crapshoot.

There's an election in November. Make your vote count. The county you save may be your own.

No Big Deal

How much actual difference will it make in our lives if we allow the mayor and her little buddies to attempt to dictate to us who we're supposed to be and how we're supposed to act?

Not much.

Norwood will remain Norwood despite June Estep's conceits and Marsha West's delusions. Marsha needs to sell something real, commercial or imagined. We should be kind and allow her to make a living at the expense of people who cherish their lifestyles in what has been a residential neighborhood for as long as it's been a neighborhood.

If our "expansion girls" relented and actually listened to what people have to say, then Marsha might make a buck and the mayor might get her point across. If the Himes and Zehm properties were zoned residential, there might be a ton of money to be made without an industrial scepter being brandished to force the local citizenry into accepting something they obviously don't want.

Who in their right mind would move an industrial outfit to Norwood? Who would want to put up with the local political scene? Serious businessmen are not political or practical shmoos. Access to markets is severely limited out of Norwood. The ranchers already know that. Besides that, we're way overpriced. If you don't believe me, ask Scott Flyrod or any number of other businesses, which relocated elsewhere. I'm certain that the 50 employees of Scott in Montrose are thankful our mayor couldn't keep them here. The only market we deal with effectively is Telluride. We already provide Telluride with service and professional personnel and can increase our capacity. There are people successfully establishing businesses out of town with good reason.

It's a good commute if you're getting paid. I know. I wouldn't deal with the Board of County Commissioners or interminable meetings of multifarious commissions or boards if I weren't getting paid. For me it's about being a professional. It's a job. On the other hand, I love to write.

Serious light industrial operation outside of town is more attractive, even with the burden of county planning to deal with, than anything the mayor can possibly offer. Hopefully, the mayor's new found sense of cooperation will allow a more civil political atmosphere, which will in turn allow people to seriously consider moving here.

No great danger we'll be over run by developers or industrial types anytime soon. Let's let the mayor have her fun.

We'll get zoned for upscale yuppie lifestyles and wind up like Basalt or El Jebel or Carbondale with cute little shops selling us stuff nobody really needs. We'll have to drink Chardonnay or Perrier for lunch. High-dollar, high-cheeked bimos with politically correct silicone implants will bore us to tears with tales of their latest vacation to Aruba. We'll have to wear Topsiders with no socks. We won't be able to find a real cup of coffee anywhere. We'll have a bridle path and a bike path for profilers in Dayglo outfits. Beer will cost $5 a glass for yuppie brew. Are you getting the picture yet?

Hunting will be allowed only if you bring a veterinarian to stitch up and save the poor critter you just shot. Everything will be registered including BB guns and slingshots. Fishing will be catch and release only since the fish in the San Miguel won't be fit to eat. You won't be able to ride a bicycle, much less a motorcycle, without a helmet.

There won't be as much water in the San Miguel by that time since logging will have been banned in the county and forests will be so thick no water will make it down the watershed into the rivers. We'll live in constant fear of firestorms. Wolves will have run of the mesas. We'll be secure and safe by BOCC resolution. Ranches will have been carved up into 35-acre, rurally clustered ranchettes. The Lone Cone Saloon will become a vegetarian brewpub. Ralph Lauren will buy the Maverick and we won't have to drive to Montrose for anything. Somebody will open a real liquor store in town and we'll finally get rid of the mayor.

Neighborhood of Strangers

Art Goodtimes will get a haircut and a shave, move into a maid-serviced condo and preach as an enlightened commodity. Anna Zivian will finally get a real job and find out what life is all about. Jim Craft will declare himself commissioner for life so he never has to pretend at being an attorney ever again. I'll go back to being a mobilist because we'll all be so politically correct and perfect there will be no more need for the press. The yups will buy my stuff for millions because they're so easy to fool.

Then we can sell out for the big money and worry about nothing but capital gains. We'll also have to figure out where to go and how to replace what we just lost.

Consider how really good we have it here now. Then consider what's being planned and is already being implemented. Stand up and be counted or sit down and relax.

It's really no big deal.

The Spirit And Intent Of The Merger

The merger agreement between the Town of Norwood, the San Miguel Conservancy Water District and the Wright's Mesa Rural Water System was created in the spirit of good will, good faith and cooperation; in an effort to improve water for everybody in the area. Unfortunately, we've lost sight of both the spirit and the letter of the agreement.

June Estep signed the agreement December 28, 1992. Bill Bray and Don Erickson signed December 29, 1992. For those of you unfamiliar with the contents of this important document, The Post is publishing the Agreement in its entirety in this issue.

The water system, prior to the agreement, was inefficient and apparently no one disagrees that the intent of the agreement was to make efficiency of management viable.

The reason to create an efficient management group was due to new federal regulations, which created new water standards. Other than the new standards, the water system, although inefficient, worked. The standards of water processing needed to be upgraded and the process required outside money. The San Miguel Water Conservancy District is a taxing entity and, in the spirit of neighborliness and cooperation, offered a helping hand in 1978. They didn't want to run a water system nor are they designed to do that. They are designed for the big picture of increasing raw water in the region.

We need to keep sight of the fact that the merger took place for more efficient management. The mechanics of equality is one of the major things the merger is about, equality between the in-town and out-of-town water users. Out-of-town users pay a majority of the costs

231

of the system but the Town of Norwood owns the assets. It hasn't been totally equitable to this point.

It was also agreed there would be separate financial accounting for the water system, separate from the town. It was an excellent idea. Unfortunately, it hasn't quite worked that way.

Section III, B11 of the agreement states: "Because the Water System will pay a significant portion of the salaries of town employees, the town will consult with the Water Commission prior to taking and personnel actions concerning those employees."

The commission was set up 3-3, in-town and out-of-town members, in an effort at equality, despite the fact that out-of-town water system subscribers pay the brunt of the costs of running the system and a good portion of the town. In case of a tie, the town board was to make decisions.

I believe that the people who wrote this document, with one notable exception, couldn't have foreseen, nor would they have agreed to have the same people who are on the commission make decisions on the town board, especially considering the fact that, to date, The Norwood Water Commission and the Norwood Board of Trustees are run by the mayor and her two cohorts. The grapevine has it that she also runs the planning commission, of which she is an ex-officio member, and has a tendency to speak for the entire town board and the town, when what she actually does is speak merely for herself with the aid of a lawyer, which we all pay for. If Estep were paying for the attorney out of her own pocket, you can bet we wouldn't have to deal with this idiocy.

The really unfortunate aspect of this is the type of personality controlling the town board. If we were to have someone trustworthy, even this situation might be workable. This is not the case presently. A dictatorial mayor, one unwilling to listen to what people have to say and want is absolutely unacceptable.

Equality for in-town and out-of-town water services was the intent of the agreement and the agreement wording supports that. Tap fees were to remain the same and water shortage to be shared equally. Water service was to remain the same.

The express agreement that the Norwood Water Commission will operate the water system has been lost sight of by the members of the town board who serve on the commission. The town board has also lost sight of that. Members of the town board have the wrong attitude toward the community at large.

Commission members, who are also town board members, have involved the water commission in things, which have absolutely no relevancy to operating a water system. That's one of the reasons there have been so many difficulties to this point. Development, zoning and planning are issues, which do not concern the water commission. The water system has no business being involved in these issues. The rural commercial water tap controversy should never have happened. It caused an inordinate amount of friction, trouble and expense. It consumed time, which could have otherwise been used to run the system more efficiently. It was a dumb thing to do. It could all have been avoided if the mayor had stuck to the deal and not tried to weasel her way out of it, despite her latest machinations to manipulate the truth.

Norwood would not exist without the contribution of the rural people. There would be no grocery store, hardware store or bank, for instance. The rural people are overwhelming contributors to the town's economic and cultural welfare.

Wright's Mesa includes Norwood, not the other way around. Our mayor, who is becoming increasingly more well known for her ability to manipulate figures and facts, last week wrote a letter to The Post stating that "At the time of the merger, the water system was $400,000 in debt. The rural system was $700,000 in debt."

The actual figures are quite different. According to the resolution of the San Miguel Water Conservancy District, signed by Bill Bray on December 12, 1992 and Don Erickson on December 29, 1992, the debt was $224,750. The approximate amount of the SMWCD was $454,000, according to the merger signed by Estep, Bray and Erickson.

Mayor Estep's figures add up to $1,100,000. The real figures add up to $678,750. That's a difference of $421,250. My invitation to the mayor to explain these discrepancies and other questions, which the public and I have, remains open. Guess what, so far she hasn't called, nor do I think she's likely to. Need I remind you that our mayor said: "Things in contracts aren't always what they seem," at a public meeting she called but couldn't control. Seems the mayor thinks everything is negotiable when she's not pleased with it. A deal is still a deal, no matter how you try to sleaze out of it.

Estep also spent $440 to advertise water restriction notices in September 1996. That's a lot of money when you consider the amount of people she had to notify. She spent $308 in the San Miguel Basin Forum and $132 in The San Miguel County Post. Where do the people who use the water live?

Perhaps our mayor has taken on too much, with all the boards she's on, all the stuff she has to control and all the questionable facts, figures and authorizations she has to keep track of. We'd all be better off if she stuck to selling liquor and helped her husband with the horses.

Have It Your Way

We all won when the commissioners last Wednesday voted to reject the town acquisition to annex rights of way in the residential neighborhood east of Norwood.

The town board won because they got a much needed reality check. The mayor won because she got a much needed reality check. Richard Grice won because he got a reality check and a quality control check.

The people who live in that neighborhood won because they stuck it out, believed in process and acted like the good neighbors and citizens they are. Good judgment and common sense triumphed.

The commissioners won because they made a good decision, listened to the people and demonstrated that representative, reactive local government works.

The entire county won because we now understand the people of Wright's Mesa and Norwood are reasonable, courteous, patient and understanding. All they require is to be listened to with some assurance that those in charge have their best interests in mind and will come to effective decisions based on fact and not on vague perception or tunnel vision ambition.

The commissioners demonstrated that reasonable government is possible. The people of Wright's Mesa demonstrated that reasonable interaction in a courteous and orderly process is possible in this end of the county. This should clear up a lot of misconception and misunderstanding.

If we use what we learned at this meeting as a basis for future interaction, we can realistically have government of, by and for the people in this county. Everyone listened, paid attention, had a turn.

It strengthened my faith in process. I am continually impressed by the heart, spirit and gumption of the residents of the West End of San Miguel County. I was impressed with the decision made by Anna Zivian and Leslie Sherlock.

My congratulations to Anna Zivian for proving wrong my prediction that the BOCC vote would be 2-1 in favor of the town. It was unusual, refreshing and historic to see Jim Craft vote alone.

There has been a problem, not only on this end of the county, with political and economic perceptions and realities. It's much ado about very little. Norwood will remain Norwood for a long while because of the people who live in town and the people who surround it. The people are one and determined to stay that way despite the political consternation and dissent caused by dictatorial personalities in local government.

Decisions have been made recently, which seem to be getting us back on track of responsible government and a realistic outlook for the future. I wouldn't recommend we return to our normally apathetic political comfort just yet. We need to keep up the pressure, attend meetings and stay in touch with what's happening on the local scene with boards, commissions and the like.

Hopefully the BOCC decision will help Mr. Grice find suitable employment elsewhere and we shall no longer be burdened with his 'expertise' or bills. There's a Grice bill for $2,244.50 for the rights of way county planning and zoning meeting in August. Enough already. It is time for Norwood leadership to reassess the real needs of the community.

There is an election coming up in less than a month. Be certain of who you want to represent you. There are candidate's forums scheduled for the entire month. There are good candidates and mediocre ones. There are candidates who represent their constituents and candidates who don't. There are candidates who tell the truth and others who dance around it because they're not familiar with this concept. Make up your mind before you step into the voting booth. Again, there are perceptions and realities to deal with here.

You can all win again if you deal with reality, the truth and take time to figure out what you actually want. If you don't have it your way, you'll have it someone else's way. Have it your way.

The Mayor's Spokespeople

So far no one has publicly called the mayor a liar to her face. I suppose that the reason for this is because of a sense of propriety, manners and besides, it just isn't done. To do so would imply that the voters who elected her were dupes or that she's so skilled that she's gone undetected for over a term. On the other hand, she has shown all the signs, tendencies, and evidence that it is true.

Of course, we in the press have had to pussyfoot around it and make excuses for her honor. The mayor is a clever girl and plays everything she can to her advantage in order to get her way.

After she shot her big mouth off in a letter, not an editorial, to the Post, getting figures and facts completely wrong, she skipped the next San Miguel Water Conservancy Board of Directors meeting because she knew she'd get called on by the rest of the board of directors who are sick and tired of the way she conducts business.

Then she got Daily Planet stringer Marie Fouche to front for her and make excuses in a story about the Norwood Town Board's most recent meeting where Fouche claims that the mayor "informed the Conservancy District that the numbers came from the recently completed audit."

There was no way that Fouche could have known where the numbers came from since she wasn't at the meeting in question to report on it. She may have gotten her information straight from the mayor. All the mayor is trying to do here is cover herself without having to take the heat for her irresponsible statements made in writing.

Fouche has reported on several meetings, which she has not attended. I did see her briefly at the BOCC works session last week. Apparently she is June Estep's personal spokesperson with little regard for reality, process or professional ethics. I can't say for sure that this is gospel but where does she get her information if she's not at the meetings she reports on?

I know about the mayor's public relations tactics with the press because I represented her exclusively while I worked for Roger Culver at the San Miguel Basin Forum. He didn't mind then, he doesn't mind now. If you want to read what the mayor's slant is on something, read the Forum.

Since the Daily Planet employs excellent writers like Eric Whitney and Bob Beer, I'm surprised publisher Tony Daryani would allow such transparent public relations efforts on the pages of the region's only daily. I constantly see Whitney and Beer both at local and regional gatherings of note. They are skilled reporters, good writers and good guys. Daryani remains questionable. Perhaps he should send Estep a bill for Fouche's advertising services.

There are a lot of people on Wright's Mesa and in Norwood who are embarrassed for and by the mayor, myself included. She won't talk with The Post because we question the "facts" she comes up with. She's still trying to "explain away" the last letter she wrote us. Could be she has nothing to say if it can be questioned.

Things must be getting hot for her honor.

What's Going On Here?

Election Day is little less than a week away. Those of you who care enough to be politically aware of issues and candidates know what's up and who and what you're voting for. Those of you who read these commentaries know I call'em the way I see'em.

From my point of view, the most important issue confronting us in the election is the commissioner candidates. It's actually very simple. There are two candidates qualified to represent us. From the 3rd District we have Republican Jim Young and from the 1st District we have Democrat Anna Zivian. That's who I'm voting for. I'm sure you'll vote for whoever you think is best. Good luck.

Now back to the mayor and the slapstick we've become accustomed to as local government, brought to us by June Estep, Ralph Weaver and Marsha West. They're the triumvirate who sit on the Norwood Town Board and the Norwood Water Commission, whose particular antics bring to mind vintage Three Stooges footage.

Estep also parades as mayor and sticks her nose into the business of Norwood Planning and Zoning Commission with the aid of her $50 an hour sidekick Richard Grice. My compliments and admiration to P&Z chair Christine Beeby for standing up to the mayor at the last P&Z meeting and speaking up for her friends and neighbors. Christine sees us as people. The mayor sees us as possible tax revenue. The mayor needs the money to keep up her outrageous, unauthorized spending habits, for which we foot the bill. Can an increase in water rates be far away?

Estep has a deal going with attorney Sherry Caloia, despite questions dealing with the propriety and legality of Calioia's hiring for the Norwood Water Commission. The questions were brought up in March of this year after Calioa was hired following executive session where rural member M.J. Cadgene had been excluded. The Three Stooges ratified Caloia's hire at the March 26 NWC meeting, totally after the fact. M.J. Cadgene abstained and Gale Ragsdale was absent. The rural sector of the NWC was not represented in this decision.

Discussions concerning Caloia's hire were made over the phone and not in public session. Estep's infamous board and commission polls were again employed. Estep became Caloia's contact and discussed commission business over the phone, in private, without benefit of public hearing or process. What the hell is going on here?

According to Colorado's Sunshine Laws, a public board or commission must cite chapter and verse of what and why something's being discussed in executive session before the session. This was not done. Decisions must be made outside the session. Estep has been hiding out in executive session, board polls and private phone calls for long enough. Let's hear it out in the open!

According to the Colorado Press Association the budget needs to be revised and updated publicly to reflect the impact of the contract discussed in executive session.

According to the town staff no budget authority for line item expenses for legal advice has been made; the Calioa contract is totally open-ended, meaning amounts could be spent on anything and there is no ceiling on lawyer expenditures. The budget has not been amended to show projected legal fees.

This is your money we're talking about, which the Three Stooges are readily spending.

There are no minutes on phone meetings, which are unauthorized.

Attorney Caloia charges $105 an hour plus $35 an hour travel time. How much money do you make an hour? Who pays you for travel time? Caloia travels from Glenwood Springs. Marsha West arranged for Caloia's hire. Caloia's open-ended "contract" was sent March 22, 1996 and approved and accepted by June Estep on March 23, 1996.

We, neighbors and friends, have been paying outrageous sums to Estep's attorney, whose hire still remains questionable. Why is Calioa still attending meetings when rural members continually question her presence? Estep has Caloia on the NWC as a seventh member to give her another advantage. Let Estep pay her own damned bills for her own damned lawyer.

As of August 31, 1996, NWC operational expenses exceeded revenue by approximately $35,000 according to Neal Snyder, rural NWC member. Snyder also maintains that $18,000 of NWC Plant Investment Fees are unaccounted for.

Town staff maintains that the NWC may have trouble meeting debt service in the coming year. Tim Lippert, Norwood Public Works Director, chose not to publish notices about the substandard quality of NWC water in the local paper. If there actually is a problem with the quality of the water here, why was Lippert on vacation while EPA standards were not being met? What is the problem with our recently refurbished water plant? Why aren't we meeting EPA standards? Are our kids drinking this substandard water in the Norwood School? Lippert answers to Ralph Weaver and Mayor June Estep. The Stooges strike again.

It is time for responsible, realistic citizens to conduct the business of local government. Estep and her cohorts, including Calioa and Grice need to hit the road and let competent people do the job.

"I'm sick and tired of your bs, June," said rural member Don Erickson at the last commission meeting. I agree.

You Get What You Give
To The Process

After a year of covering meetings, work sessions, commissions, boards and a variety of governmental, semi-governmental and civic functions, I find that it's all much ado about very little.

Development happens. It is a fact of life that there are more and more people in the world every minute. These people and their families require some place to live other than the place they have already screwed up past recognition. People with money move here because it's cool, hip, politically correct and in.

Economics happens. Everybody needs a job sooner or later. Whether you have to drive to Telluride or not is of very little consequence to anyone other than yourself. If you have a job in Telluride you're probably thankful that the rent gets paid and there's groceries. It would be nice if you could work closer to home but you go where the money is.

Money talks. This is obvious.

Attitudes change. When people move into this or any other area, they bring their own attitudes with them. When people who move into an area have more money, more power and more influence, then attitudes change in their direction because they do what they jolly well please. If you don't like it, you can do what you jolly well please too.

It isn't fair. So what. Fair relies heavily on what side of the money talks discussion you represent. There is a second half to the money talks statement.

There's got to be some way to stop this. There isn't. This isn't a discussion of whether we're going to have development but how. The same applies to economic attitudes and fairness.

I have nothing against development, growth and economic opportunity. It's fine by me. I think it would be just great if all the people of this area, and I mean Wright's Mesa, could have jobs right here. By now you probably know how I feel about the Norwood Bridge.

What I do have a problem with is how our elected and appointed officials deal with process. There seems to be a near-total disregard for process here. There is also a near-total lack of participation on the part of local citizens.

If you're not happy with what is happening, then speak up, voice your opinion, participate! In this past year of reporting I have noticed an obvious lack of participation at meetings, which affect pocketbooks and lifestyles of everybody in town. One notable exception has been school board meetings. The rest of local governmental functions are virtually ignored except by a few diehards who don't live in town. If you don't participate then you deserve what you're served.

No wonder our local politicos feel they've got a mandate from some nebulous silent majority. We have a second-term mayor by acclamation. Nobody else ran. Nobody shows up at meetings. Oh, they'll get hot under the collar once the process is over and nothing can be done except complain. The citizens are good at that.

Norwood's infamous "Kitchen Cabinet" do as they damn well please, because they're aware that the people of this town are apathetic and not likely to do anything. Could be our elected and appointed officials are genius visionaries who will bring peace, prosperity and harmony to Wright's Mesa. We've already given them the benefit of the doubt.

So far we're in major-league debt with a water system, which can't deliver substandard water through crumbling infrastructure. But we do have a brand-spanking new reservoir. And we have a recently refurbished water treatment plant, which can't handle treating water to EPA specifications. This is all going to cost more money despite the fact that the price of water has gone up 60% in the last two years. This whole economic fiasco is being based on transparent water tap projections.

Neighborhood of Strangers

So far, during the tenure of our present leadership, we have lost the San Miguel County Law Enforcement Center, Scott Flyrod, and are in danger of losing the USFS headquarters. Between the jail and Scott alone there's approximately 75 jobs lost to this area. That's quite an economic impact. Where was our local leadership when opportunity beat feet and hit the road? They certainly were ready with excuses as to whose fault it was. We need results and opportunity, not excuses. Luckily, there are people in this area who do pay attention, face reality and create opportunity, no thanks to local leadership.

A good step in the right direction might be to consider open meetings, public input, actual dissemination of information, adherence to the Colorado Open Meetings Law, respect for process, respect for what the people want and a realistic, fiscally responsible plan for the future. We need to re-establish trust. The people need to participate. Without participation and trust our system doesn't work.

You get what you give. You deserve what you get.

What's Ailing Us!

If you consider the boards and commissions on Wright's Mesa that are in turmoil, then you will recognize one name common to all—June Estep, Norwood's mayor. Think about it. Everywhere there's trouble June Estep is involved.

There's trouble with the Norwood Water Commission, trouble with the San Miguel Water Conservancy District, trouble with the Norwood Town Board, trouble with the Norwood Planning and Zoning Commission, trouble everywhere June Estep is involved. Do we actually need all this trouble?

At the last meeting of the Norwood Water Commission June Estep publicly stated that her newspaper is the San Miguel Basin Forum. June is a town and rural water subscriber to the Norwood Water Commission. She hustles liquor in Norwood. She can read whatever she likes. The mayor isn't happy with The Post because we call her on the manure she tries to pass off as responsible government.

The reason Estep picks the Forum for her paper is that she has her way, without threat of being questioned or checked in the Forum. They print what she has to say verbatim. This is not real journalism. This is advertising, public relations and show business. Apparently June has been steering a few ads to the Forum. Money talks. They're not an ambitious publication.

Estep has a problem with dysfunction. If you disagree with her then you're declared dysfunctional, when all you're doing is stating your opinion. After a year of covering boards and commissions I have found the mayor to have a tendency to get quite out of her mind if you are not in total agreement with what she tries to put over on you. Just watch her jaws get tight and locked into a knot when she is challenged.

Look out. The level of her whine increases and the arrogance emerges. It's a junkyard dog mentality.

It's clear Estep needs to be in charge of everything. Either she's terminally insecure or else she has no faith in what people want. The voters of Norwood made a big mistake when they elected her and an even bigger mistake when they didn't challenge her. The voters of this town are obviously oblivious. The people of Wright's Mesa aren't.

Before June Estep became mayor there was no difference between people. Now there is. There's town people and rural people. The people who have businesses in town but residences out of town have no say about what happens in town. It was never a problem until Estep. The dissension and problems on the mesa about water, zoning and annexation emerged with June Estep. Estep's ambitions, which by the way we are funding, are at the heart of what's ailing us. There was no problem between the town and the Farmers Water Development Company before Estep. When Norwood needed water the farmers pitched in and helped. It's a recorded fact. Cooperation was the norm on Wright's Mesa before she took over. She fixed that while she was trying to gain control over regional water.

The infrastructure of the water system is virtually in the same sad shape it was when she took over four years ago. The refurbished water plant is still not adequate. The water commission has more water than it can store or use and she's still trying to get more. Estep is at war with the San Miguel Water Conservancy District, Farmers Water Development Company, and half of the Norwood Water Commission. If she wasn't at war with all of these people, who have lived neighborly, reasonable and cooperative lives, there would be no need for her to hire lawyers. We're in debt over $2 million since Estep went on her binge.

Estep hired Sherry Caloia, a lawyer from Glenwood Springs, with town board and water commission money. Calioa has been writing our resolutions. She is writing our letters. She is telling us what to do and how to do it at public meetings. This woman is at least as arrogant as our mayor. Her credibility as an employee of the water commission is questionable. She doesn't just give advice when asked. She shoots her mouth off like a member of the commission or the board whenever she feels like it.

Are the people on our boards and commissions so inept that they can't write letters or resolutions or work out their differences in the spirit of neighborly and civic cooperation? Do we really need to hire an extra board and commission member at $105 per hour? Sherry Caloia should keep her mouth shut until somebody asks her a question having to do with legal advice. Better yet, she should stay in Glenwood. Are there no lawyers in San Miguel County with water experience? Think of the money we'd save on travel time!

Estep is a welcome mat for urban expectations. She sees Norwood as a mega-development project akin to the Roaring Fork Valley. We're situated between Telluride and Moab. It's an obvious parallel. The major stumbling block to Estep's ambitions is the lack of water. Why else would she be after more when we already have more than enough? Why did she hire a lawyer from Glenwood, familiar with development and water in the Roaring Fork Valley?

June Estep is a capable, intelligent, strong-willed arrogant woman, who could do tons of good for Norwood and the region if she'd just listen to the people who have lived here all along. She's not hard of hearing, just hard of understanding. She doesn't need to go to war with everybody.

Instead of speculating on the future, she might consider dealing with the present, with reality, with getting what we have under control before we embark on a plan most of us aren't privy to, which seems so obvious to her. We may agree with it or not but we should deal with it together.

Months ago I called June Estep and offered to interview her so she could present her side of the story in order to clear the air and clarify whatever misunderstandings she might consider. I did this in the spirit of respect and cooperation. June said she'd think about it and let me know what she has decided. She never has. The offer remains open.

L'Chaim

The mayor never calls.

Peter Spencer quietly advertises The San Miguel County Post for sale In The New York Times. He sells The Post to Robert Chickering, a symphony bass player from Maine who doesn't have a clue about the 5 W's, how to write a lead, how to load film in camera or how to run a newspaper. Cynthia Hansen-Zehm, the astrology writer for The Post, tells me on the street, before it is officially announced that Spencer had sold the paper. I ask Peter why he hadn't told me. "Because you'd have quit," is his reply. I'm sold along with the assets.

Chickering takes the paper over with the August 28, 1996 issue. Peter Spencer goes to work as spokesman for San Miguel Power and continues writing his Fearless Leader column in The Post. Working with Chickering is more than I am willing to deal with. I last a few months and quit. In the Yiddish vernacular of the neighborhood I grew up in, Chickering is a putz.

I'm 51 years old with a voice of my own and it's finally time to write a book. I live on potato pancakes and coffee, on the big risk to see if I have the stuff to be a gainfully unemployed writer. I like potato pancakes and coffee.

On April 2, 1997, The San Miguel County Post declares: "CITIZENS FILE RECALL PETITON FOR MAYOR."

The recall committee: Joe Vigil, Betty Odle, Chuck Heldman and Mike Grafmeyer present a petition to recall June Estep, Marsha West, Autumn Crutcher, Ralph Weaver and Carmie Richeson.

Grounds for recall against Estep: "lack of appreciation, consideration, and responsiveness to information and opinion of the electors and the community; excessive and expensive use of and reliance on professional advisors to the exclusion and disregard of the advice, opinion, and information provided by the electors and the community; taking action on many matters before giving adequate consideration thereto and notice to electors to the community; and lack of fiscal responsibility."

The same exact grounds are cited for West, Crutcher, Weaver, and Richeson with this addition: "lack of independent thinking and judgment." Colorado Sunshine Statute 31-4-503 is cited.

Chickering writes that in the 3-year period up to this point, $115,702 was spent on lawyers and planners but only $2,002 was spent on youth, parks, and recreation; and that "These expenditures were not previously published, in addition to all bills, by the Town of Norwood, as required by state statute." (31-20-202)

The San Miguel County Post, in a special edition on July 2, 1997 declares: "RECALL RESULTS—62% YES". The Norwood Town Board is recalled by a more than 2-1 margin: Estep 106-47, Crutcher 104-49, Richesin 102-50, Weaver 97-56, West 110-42.

Gene Cross is sworn is as mayor, Town Planner Richard Grice resigns, most of Norwood P&Z resign.

The San Miguel County Post on July 16, 1997 announces that the town, NWC, and SMWCD all harmoniously work out an agreement to the 1992 merger agreement that satisfies everyone, no lawyers required.

Bill Bray, president of the SMWCD presents wishes of the SMWCD that Estep, West, and Weaver be banned for 25 years from serving on the Norwood Water Commission.

You can fight City Hall. Peace on Wright's Mesa again. The neighborhood is a little less strange. They still have Telluride glitz and big money foolishness to deal with but 35 miles, tradition and time will heal even that.

Peter Spencer and I were serious about The San Miguel County Post's motto: "Journalism Is The First Draft Of History - An Informed Electorate Is The Foundation Of Democracy."

Peter Spencer died in Telluride on February 15, 1999. He was born in Brooklyn, NY, on January 18, 1939. He graduated from Yale University in 1960 with a degree in English literature. After graduation, Peter worked in the textile industry in North Carolina, where he and an associate revolutionized the industry by interfacing knitting machines with computers. Spencer set up Telluride's first computer system in 1979. He served as Telluride's mayor from 1989 to 1992.

At Peter's funeral I stand by a San Miguel County Post vending machine at graveside, mourning the loss of my friend, mentor and the only editor I got along with in 40 years as a journalist. Peter Spencer helped launch the best writing run of my life, which continues.

Tailings from the Tomboy Mine continue to leach traces of Telluride's hard rock mining past into the San Miguel River. Dirk DePagter hustles real estate in the world-class ski area he envisioned and helped create. He saw his children and grandchildren grow up in Telluride. Bill Masters is still Sheriff of San Miguel County. Doris Ruffe and Darryl Elder died. June Estep moved.

Peter Spencer's headstone proclaims L'CHAIM.

About the Author

O.Z. Lysiak is a beach addict. He lives in a barn on the Oregon Coast with his wife Christina, and two local mutts. Lysiak is devoted to clarity, writing and making mobiles.